Sw

'He lay with his head on his arm and he no longer felt the cold of the stone beneath him. He knew that he should be on his feet yelling into the night, but he couldn't yell any more; he was too tired, he was all in. As he went to sleep he wondered if he would ever see his mother again. This was what she had feared, him getting lost on the hills. It was funny about that. Yes, it was very funny when he came to think about it. That had been her great fear, that if he went camping or tramping he'd get lost and die on some mountain. It was funny . . . funny the way things turned out. She must have had one of those premonitions, sort of.'

Matty Doolin has one ambition in life – to work with animals. But his parents don't understand him, and insist that Matty should follow his father into the docks. A camping holiday on a farm high in the fells leads Matty into unexpected danger – but finally into a new and satisfying way of life.

MATTY DOOLIN
CATHERINE COOKSON

CORGI BOOKS

MATTY DOOLIN
A CORGI BOOK 0 552 52526 X

Originally published in Great Britain by
Macdonald, London

PRINTING HISTORY
Macdonald edition published 1965
Corgi edition published 1989
Corgi edition reprinted 1989 (twice)

This book is set in 11/12 pt Century textbook
by Colset Private Limited, Singapore.

Corgi Books are published by Transworld Publishers
Ltd., 61–63 Uxbridge Road, Ealing, London W5 5SA, in
Australia by Transworld Publishers (Australia) Pty. Ltd.,
15–23 Helles Avenue, Moorebank, NSW 2170, and in New
Zealand by Transworld Publishers (N.Z.) Ltd., Cnr. Moselle
and Waipareira Avenues, Henderson, Auckland.

Printed and bound in Great Britain by
Cox & Wyman Ltd., Reading, Berks.

MATTY DOOLIN

1

'Doolin! Did you hear what I said?'

'Yes, sir.'

'What did I say?'

Matty Doolin's thick-set body made an uneasy movement. The seat of his desk was pressing against the back of his knees – it always did when he stood up – but if he should step out into the aisle and stand straight old Bore would, as usual, say, 'Going some place, Doolin?'

'Well, come along, I'm waiting.'

'You were talkin' about stellar conglomerations, sir.' Matty wasn't surprised at himself for remembering that mouthful, because his mother was always using the word conglomeration. 'Look at all this conglomeration,' she would say when she came into his room in the morning, or, 'Get that conglomeration off the table; I want to set the tea.' But she used the word most when referring to Nelson, and somehow Matty didn't think it fitted in this last case because Nelson was just one thing. Well, not a thing; Nelson was his dog. She misused the word conglomeration a lot when she talked of Nelson. 'Get that conglomeration outside!' 'Look at the conglomeration of dirt on my floor from that beast's feet!' The thought of Nelson disturbed Matty. And then there was the pain in the back of his legs. And

7

now Mr Borley's voice was coming at him again, sharp-edged with sarcasm. 'Stellar conglomerations ... I would say you were about' – the master paused and looked ceilingwards before again dropping his narrow lids in Matty's direction – 'about one light year behind us, Doolin. Since you took your attention from us we have traversed quite a bit of the sky, but now that you have deigned to give us your attention once more do you think you can name one globular cluster which is visible to the naked eye? You might remember we spoke of these at the beginning of the lesson.'

Matty's chin jerked, causing a strand of his thick red hair to fall across his brow. He pushed it upwards out of his eyes as if to give him a better view of the master, and he hesitated a moment before saying in a tight voice, 'Century.'

'Century?' repeated the master, making a small motion with his head. 'I thought you would remember that one. But it is not Century, Doolin, it is Cen-tauri, Centauri. Would you like to repeat that?'

'Centauri.' The word seemed to have to struggle through Matty's tight lips. His whole face felt tight, as did his body; it always went like that when he was angry. He had a desire to step out into the aisle, square his shoulders, and walk boldly up to the undersized, pasty-faced Mr Borley and say, 'Who are you going to torment next term, because in just four weeks' time I'll be gone?' He hated Borley; he was the only master in the school he disliked. He would have liked school if it hadn't been for Borley; he would have also liked astronomy lessons, because he liked looking at the sky.

'Sit down.'

8

Matty did not immediately respond to the master's bark, and before he sat down he lowered his head and looked towards his desk. And he was still looking at the desk when he felt the soft nudge in his thigh. Joe, who sat next to him, always made this sympathetic gesture after old Bore had been doing his stuff.

Joe Darling and he had been pals all through their school days. They had started in the primary school together.

Matty realized he was going to miss Joe when they left school, but that was his own fault because he could do the same as Joe was going to do, he could go in the yards part-time and attend the Technical School part-time. But he didn't want to go into the ship-yards, or the mines, and he wasn't cut out for an office. Oh, he knew that he wasn't cut out for an office. Well, what did he want to do? He didn't know, not really . . . but yes, he did; yes, he knew all right. But could he tell Mr Funnell?

After this lesson he was due to go and talk to Mr Funnell again. The careers master had been very patient; he had suggested all kinds of things, except the one thing that Matty knew in his heart he wanted to be. Mr Funnell hadn't mentioned that because probably it hadn't dawned on him that Matty Doolin wanted to be a vet, because Mr Funnell knew, and he knew, you had to have a certain education to be a vet. A love of animals wasn't enough.

'All right, you can go . . . AND QUIETLY!'

Matty eased himself out of his seat and joined the throng in the aisle, and no one spoke until they were passing from the classroom into the wide corridor. And here Matty received a dig in the ribs which came with a hoarse whisper, 'Old

9

Bore loves you, Ginger Doormat, doesn't he?'

With the quickness of a judo expert Matty turned on his tormentor and a nothing-barred fight seemed imminent, but it was strangled at its source by the incisive voice of Mr Borley saying, 'You're asking for trouble, aren't you, Doolin? And you Cooper? Break it up.'

Bill Cooper dashed towards the playground while Matty, accompanied by Joe, followed more slowly.

'You shouldn't take any notice,' said Joe; 'he just does it to get your back up. He's as bad as old Bore. It's funny, you know, about nicknames, Matty, 'cos you don't rise when you're called Ginger or Doormat separate, just when they're put together. I can't see the difference meself. And anyway it's nothing really, man. What would you do if you were stuck with a name like mine, Darlin', and all the ways they say it? Joe Darlin', JOE DARLIN', Joe DARLIN'.' Joe mimicked the way his name was pronounced. 'At first it made me want to fight, and I did in the Primary, as you know, but when I came up here I realized ... well, you can have a punch like a boxer, but it's not much use if a bloke as big as Bill Cooper comes at you, and me my size. So I just let them get on, and I make meself laugh when they shout Joe Darlin'. And that's what you should do, Matty, make yourself laugh.'

'Oh, shut up, man. Laugh at Cooper? It's him that'll be laughin', and on the other side of his face. I'll have it out with him afore I leave, you'll see.'

When Matty continued past the door that led into the school-yard Joe pulled at his arm, saying, 'Here, where are you going?'

'I'm to see Mr Funnell.'

'What, again?'

10

'Aye, again.'

'Well, you can do it after school; he usually sees them after school.'

'He said I had to come along at break.'

'Well you haven't anything fresh to tell him, have you?'

'No.' Matty poked his chin down towards his friend. 'So I'd better go and tell him that, hadn't I?'

Joe gazed up for a moment into the large grey eyes; then, a grin spreading across his face, he said, 'Huh! I can't make you out.'

'Well, don't strain yourself tryin'.'

On this and with a shake of his head, Matty turned from his friend and made his way along the corridor and to the room where he was to see the careers master.

On knocking upon the door and being told to enter Matty did as he was bidden, and was greeted from behind a paper-strewn desk by a tall, thin man with a face that spread upwards over the top of his head, which, but for the merest fringe behind his ears, was devoid of hair, which earned him the obvious nickname of Curly.

Matty liked Curly. You could talk to Curly, at least as much as you could talk to any schoolmaster, for schoolmasters were like dads, and most mams, they were nearly always old, and they weren't with it. There were some who tried to be with it, like Joe's mam, but they only made themselves look silly and got talked about.

'Sit down, Matty.'

Matty sat down.

'Well now.' Mr Funnell folded his arms on the desk and bent his body over them in the direction of Matty, saying as he did so, 'Well now, have you done any more thinking?'

11

'No, sir. Well, I mean things are just the same; I've got no further.'

'Why don't you make your mind up to go into the shops? If you put your mind to it you'll swim through, once you get interested in it. And you'll still be at school, sort of, half-time.'

Matty looked down at his joined hands and said quietly, 'But I'm not interested, sir, and I know I'll never be, not in the docks.'

'Well.' Mr Funnell drew himself upwards and there was now a touch of sharpness in his voice as he said, 'You could do much worse. You'd be learning a trade, and later on you'd have some sort of security. Whereas, standing from where I see you now, you're going to end up as a labourer . . . Perhaps that's what you want?'

'It isn't.' The retort came so definitely that Mr Funnell was surprised.

'No?' Mr Funnell leant back in his chair; then added, 'Well, it's evident that you have something in mind; why don't you tell me what it is?'

'Because it's no use.' Matty's chin was working overtime now, thrusting itself upwards as if to emphasize the hopelessness of the situation.

'Leave me to be a judge of that. Just come into the open and tell me what's on your mind, eh?'

Matty's chin stopped working, his head drooped, his eyes once again looked down at his hands, and he said, below his breath, 'I wanted to be a vet. I always have.'

'Oh.' It was a small surprised sound that Mr Funnell made, but when he again said 'Oh' it was more solid sounding as if it meant business. 'Well now,' he went on, 'why haven't you brought this up before? If you knew what you wanted to be, why haven't you got down to it, and worked and

12

got your G.C.E? I'm sure you could have done it. But . . . but now it's a little late in the day . . .'

'I know, I know.' Matty's head was jerking again, but he was looking straight across the table towards the master. 'It was no use going into it, sir, because me dad wasn't for it. He said it would take five or seven years to train for it, and even if I did get a grant I'd still need money and clothes and things, and he hadn't it.'

'Yes. Yes, I see. But still it isn't the end of the world in that line. I take it by all this that you're interested in animals?'

'Yes, sir; very much, sir.'

'Very well then, you could train for the P.D.S.A., you could run a pet shop, or better still, to my mind, you could work on a farm. And who knows, one day you might have your own. It isn't an unheard-of thing . . .'

'It's no good, sir,' Matty put in.

'Don't keep saying that, Doolin.' The master's tone was sharp. 'Of course it won't be any good if you don't make a fight for what you want.'

Matty, whose eyes had again been cast down, raised them and said quietly, 'You don't know me dad, sir.'

The master returned Matty's gaze; then said quietly, 'No, I don't. Is there trouble at home?'

'Trouble?' Matty screwed up his face. 'No, no. Not that kind of trouble, sir.' He shook his head. 'Not between me mam and dad, or anything else like that. No, no.' His voice rose higher. 'It's . . . well, it's just that he's stubborn, set-like, can't see beyond his nose. I told him I wanted to work on a farm, and he said don't be daft, where are the farms around here. He said the nearest one was miles out in the country, and when I said I knew that and what about it, for if I got a job I'd be

13

living in, he said I was going to do no living in, me mam wouldn't hear of me leaving home when I was fifteen. And so that was that.'

'Do you think it would do any good if I had a word with him?'

Matty shook his head slowly. 'No, sir, I don't, not with me dad.'

'Is he against you going into the yard as an apprentice, like Joe Darling is going to do?'

'In a sort of way yes, sir, for he keeps saying, start at the bottom and you'll get there. If there's anything in you you'll get there. But I keep tellin' him, you can't get any place the day unless you have certificates and things. Not that I want to go on the scheme, I told you, Mr Funnell. But me dad just wants me to get a full-time job and start earning good money straightaway. He's in the docks himself, you see.'

Mr Funnell shook his head. Then leaning across the table towards Matty, he said, 'As I see it, your best plan is to keep pegging away at this farm idea, and if you can bring your father round to your way of thinking I might be able to help you here. You know, there's a Y.M.C.A. scheme. It takes boys, like you in your position, and gives them an eight weeks' training. You don't get any pay, just five shillings pocket money. It's an intensive course. And then they find you a job on a farm where you live in and work under the direction of the farmer, or his manager, and you learn all there is to know, and the keener you are the better it is for you. This scheme operates all over the country. I could set about making enquiries for you, that is' – he smiled – 'if you can bring your mother and father around to see it your way.'

'It sounds fine, sir.' Matty was smiling now, and the smile took the solemn, bored look from his features and gave to his face a brightness and a particular attractiveness that could not have been guessed at from his usual expression. But like a cloth being wiped over the blackboard to erase the chalk, Matty passed his hand over his face, and his smile was gone.

'They'll never let me,' he said.

'Keep on trying. There's three weeks before the end of term, a lot can happen in three weeks. Come and see me next Friday. Go along now.' Mr Funnell smiled at him, and Matty, getting to his feet, stood looking down at the master for a moment before he muttered, 'Thank you, sir, it's kind of you to bother.'

'I'm paid for it.' Mr Funnell chuckled deeply, and Matty turned from him and left the room, thinking, Aye, they're all paid for it, paid for teaching, but some do it different to others.

It was as Matty, accompanied by Joe, left the school side-gate and walked along by the wall that a head popped up from its hiding place and a fal-setto voice cried, 'Nighty-night, Doolin Darlin'.'

This interplay with their names was like a red rag to a bull to Matty. Joe might be able to stand it but he couldn't. With a bound he was over the low wall and on top of Bill Cooper. With one arm he pinned Bill's shoulder, with the other he did his best to bring his fist into contact with Bill's nose. But Bill Cooper was a match in strength for Matty, and the next moment it was Matty who had his back to the pavement and Bill who was on top. But only for a second, for Matty's fighting spirit was being fanned by his burning indigna-tion against this big hulking boy, who usually did

15

his fighting with his tongue, and then made a run for it.

It was at the same instant that Matty felt his coat sleeve ripping from his left shoulder that he swung his right arm, fist doubled, and had the sweet satisfaction of feeling it making contact with Bill Cooper's face. Also he knew for a certainty that he was winning, and this gave him the power once more to free his arm with the intention of repeating his punch. But this he never achieved, for his arm was gripped in mid-air and he was borne backwards, and there was wrenched from him a cry of agony that blotted out the face of Mr Borley.

'Get up!'

Matty struggled to his feet, then stumbled across the yard.

'Where do you think you're going?'

Matty did not answer, he just wanted to lean against the railings for he was sick with the pain in his arm. He did not as yet know what damage Bill Cooper's fists and feet had wrought on him, but he did know that Cooper had inflicted nothing to equal the wrench that Mr Borley had given to his arm.

'Get up, Cooper. Who started this?'

'He did, sir.' Bill Cooper pointed a shaking finger at Matty. 'He jumped on me from behind the wall.'

'What have you got to say, Doolin?'

Matty blinked his eyes tightly before stretching them and looking at Mr Borley. He wished it was the end of term. He wished he had left school. He knew what he would say to him then, but now he said, 'Yes, I jumped on him.'

'Oh, you did, did you?' Mr Borley did not seem at all pleased at Matty's straightforward answer.

'Well, my brave man, you'll be at the head's office at nine o'clock on Monday morning and you'll see how high he can jump on you and how hard he can come down with the stick. It'll be a pleasure to see you get your deserts, Doolin. Now get off before I attempt to take the law into my own hands.'

Matty continued to look at the master, and he wished from the bottom of his heart that Mr Borley would give way to his temptation.

'Get going.'

Slowly Matty turned away, with the thought uppermost in his mind at the moment that it was funny that Bill Cooper should be on report with most of the masters except old Bore. The saying 'Birds of a feather' surely fitted there.

'Are you feelin' all right, Matty?' Joe was walking by his side now, and he poked his head round to the front and looked up at his friend as they left the vicinity of the school.

'Aye, I'm all right.'

'Your coat sleeve's had it at the back.'

'What?' Matty looked towards his shoulder. Coo! this would set his mam off. She had bought the coat for him only a few weeks ago because he had grown so fast out of his other one. Oh lord! She would go round the bend. The thought made him spurt forward, and Joe, trotting to keep up with him, exclaimed, 'What's the hurry now? You'll likely get it when you get in.'

'I want the worst over afore me dad comes in from work. If me mam has cooled down by then she'll deal with him.' He paused; then added, 'You needn't come back with me.'

'But, but I want to.' The two boys stood looking at each other for a moment. Then Matty, biting on his lip, hurried on once more. Of course he

17

knew Joe would want to come home with him, for there would be nobody in his house until six o'clock. His mother had stopped giving him the key after she found out he took his mates in and made them tea.

The boys now went past the Dean's Hospital, then turned into Stanhope Road, past the Park, then along the road where Matty turned off into his own street, Brinkburn Street.

Matty had lived in Brinkburn Street for eleven of his fifteen years; he could remember no other home. Up till recently he had liked Brinkburn Street. It mightn't be as posh as Talbot Road, or any of the other roads that ran off Stanhope Road, but because it was where his home was he had liked it, and at times he felt called upon to defend it. But he had to admit to himself that his liking for his home and the street had faded a little during the past months. He could almost go back to the day when the process began. It was one Sunday during last Autumn when Mr Tollet, who lived across the road and whose higher social status was marked by his car which was parked every night opposite his front door, had taken his mam and dad and himself for a ride into the country, the real country, miles away. And for the first time he had seen fells, and hills as big as mountains, and great stretches of water, so clean and clear that the sky showed deep down in them and never seemed to touch bottom. It was from this day that the brightness of his home and the excitement of his street began to dim. Even the fascination of the ships crowding the jetties and filling the docks, and sailing out between South Shields and North Shields piers into the stark, bleak North Sea faded. Even living in a town that offered the excitement of great stretches of sand, of fantastic rocks, of a big football ground, of dog racing, lost its appeal ... He could think of nothing but the country, for in the country there were animals. He wanted to work with animals, tend them, help them, care for them. He did not think 'love them', because that would be cissy, but there was a feeling in him that searched for a word that implied the same as love.

The process of finding out what he really wanted to do had been painful to Matty. His thinking had been confused; he even felt frightened at times wondering why he couldn't be like the other lads, like Joe, and Willie Styles, his other pal, and go and serve his time. He knew he looked tough; and he sounded tough, except when he was talking to his dad. He knew better than to sound tough then. So this strange feeling for animals and the country and open fields did seem a bit odd. There had been a period when he made a valiant effort to make himself see sense and act normal like the other lads. That was until Nelson appeared on the scene.

Nelson had come into his life one night after school when his mother had sent him with a message to a friend of hers in Eldon Street. He had gone down the Dock way, and it was as he walked by the Dock wall that he saw the dog limping along the gutter. There was something wrong with one of its front paws, also one of its eyes looked blurred. He bent over it, and without hesitation, because he was quite unafraid of dogs, he put his hand on its head and spoke to it. The dog had started, in an odd kind of way, as if to avoid a blow. Then it had turned its head right around and looked up at Matty; and when he touched its leg it yelped but made no attempt to snap at him. The dog was without a collar, and Matty knew

19

this could mean one of many things. Perhaps it was old, or had become a nuisance, and the people had thrown it out, or perhaps they wouldn't pay the licence, or couldn't feed it; or likely they just didn't want to be bothered with it when it was hurt. There were people like that.

This wasn't the first time that Matty had handled stray dogs, but it was the first time that he had felt as angry about one, and that peculiar painful emotion, that as yet he could not define as compassion, had swamped him as he looked on this dog that was both lame and half-blind.

On this occasion Matty knew he had to do something. But what? If he took the dog home he knew what the result would be; he had tried that before. Yet he couldn't leave the poor beast here; anything could happen to it. If a gang of rough-necks got hold of it, it would be sport for them. It was this last thought that made him decide to chance taking the dog home. He would hide it in the shed, and tomorrow, being Saturday, he would take it to the P.D.S.A. and have it put to sleep. He did not think of taking it to the police station. If the police took in all the stray dogs in the town there would be no room in the lock-up for anyone else, he knew that.

So it was on this night of Matty's decision to befriend a stray dog that the course of his life was set.

'Come on,' Matty had said to the dog. But the animal had no need to be bidden to follow its new owner, for he, too, had made a decision; he liked the feel of the hand that had stroked him; moreover, he liked the smell of this boy. He would go wherever he went.

Matty and his newly acquired friend duly arrived home. But his hope of hiding the dog in the shed at the bottom of the yard proved fruit-less, for after leaving the animal with a warning to be quiet, he had hardly got through the kitchen door before a high-pitched wail followed him.

Matty's memory did not dwell on the tussle that followed against the combined force of his mother and father. Solely because of the fact that the dog was to be there for one night only, before being taken to its peaceful end on the following day, did they allow it to be kept in the shed.

Of course there are always two sides to everything, and Mrs Doolin had grounds for her opposition towards the dog, for over the past years she had found many strange animals, not only in the shed, but kept under her son's bed. Mr Doolin, on the other hand, was opposed to keeping animals on the principle that you shouldn't keep an animal unless you had room for it.

But it was Mr Doolin who gave the dog its name. Because of its infirmities he had immediately named it Nelson, and he seemed amused by his choice.

Matty, taking advantage of his father's attitude, forgot to take Nelson to the P.D.S.A. the following day, although his mother threatened what his father would do to him when he got in.

The day being Saturday, his father was slightly mellow when he came in from work; also it being Saturday, the one day in the week he had a bet on, his mellowness did not evaporate after the last race when his horse won. These were the small events that reprieved Nelson, at least temporarily.

All might have gone smoothly if Nelson had been content to stay in the shed all day, but Nelson, after tasting the warmth and comfort of the kitchen, and the smells and tit-bits forthcoming there, found the shed, in spite of the packing case and old blankets, a very dreary place; and being a really intelligent animal, he discovered how he could bring about his release almost instantaneously. He had only to sit back on his haunches, lift his head and let rip a great howl from the elongated depths of him. But what Nelson didn't understand, and what Matty tried to impress upon him, was that his howling would bring about the end of him . . .

It was as Matty now approached his street that the faint, but unmistakable eerie wail halted his step, and that of Joe. The boys looked at each other for a moment; then simultaneously they dashed up the back lane. As Matty neared his own back door the intermittent wailing became louder, and when he burst into the back-yard it caused his face to screw up in protest. But when his hand touched the latch of the shed the wailing stopped; and there to greet him when he opened the door was Nelson.

Nelson was undoubtedly an old dog. He was also, unmistakably, a mongrel, as his parents had obviously been. He was neither labrador, collie, spaniel, nor bull terrier, but a little of each. But Matty's attention to him, coupled with good feeding over the past few weeks and his own overwhelming love for this new master whose touch was soft, had brought back to him what seemed like a second childhood.

'Stop it, man. Stop it.' Matty tried to stop the dog jumping all over him at once. 'You'll get me hung, both of us hung, for I've told you, haven't I, it'll be the end of you.' He got down on his hunkers and let the dog wash his face; and Joe, also on his hunkers now, remarked as he watched Nelson's antics, 'He goes daft when he sees you, doesn't he? Are you going to take him indoors now?'

Slowly Matty pulled himself upright, then turned and looked up the yard towards the kitchen window. His mother, he realized, hadn't come to the door threatening what was going to happen to Nelson, or telling him the neighbours had all been complaining. 'Come on,' he said quietly, and together the two boys, with the dog bounding round them, went up the narrow yard and into the kitchen. At least, they got as far as the scullery door which led into the kitchen, for from there Matty saw his mother.

Mrs Doolin was standing to the side of the kitchen table in a waiting position, her arms folded across her waist. Matty stared at her in amazement for a moment. Then, his eyes moving from her stiff face, he was amazed no longer at her expression, for there, arrayed on the table in a straight line, were the remains of his father's slippers. They had been very old slippers to begin with, but now they were hardly recognizable. Next to them was a shredded tea-towel; and next to the tea-towel was a smaller mass of chewed paper. It was a browny colour. And next to this was his mother's felt hat. The hat was intact except for a piece of the brim.

'Well!'

Matty looked back at his mother. He stared at her for some time before gasping, 'Oh lor!'

'You can say that again.' Now his mother's quiet demeanour vanished and, turning to the table, she picked up one article after the other, crying, 'Look at this lot. Look at them! Your dad's slippers. You're in for something there. And a good tea-towel. But this is worse.' She picked up the small brown, pulpy mass. 'His

23

coupons, his football coupons that were going off this morning. And look at my hat . . . Well!' She wagged her head in wide movements. 'He's done for himself this time. And you, me lad' – now she thrust her fingers almost into Matty's face – 'you won't be able to talk him out of where he's going.'

'But, Mam, it's only 'cos he's lonely. If you'd only let him stay in the kitchen he'd be as quiet as a mouse. Look at him now.' Matty made rapid movements with his hand towards the dog lying peacefully on the mat before the fire.

His mother had taken up her cool stance again. 'Where do you think he was when he did this lot? They're not kept in the shed, are they? I promised you I'd keep him in, and anyway I couldn't stand Mrs Wright and all the neighbours coming to the back door complaining about him howling. This happened when I left him to go out for me shopping. He did this in an hour and a half. Moreover, he was howling in here.' She thumbed the floor. 'Comfortably ensconced on the chair there I left him, and when I came back he was howling blue murder. And this' – she swept her arm over the table – 'greeted me. If I'd been another five minutes I bet he'd have had the cushions off the couch. Well . . .' Mrs Doolin paused. 'This is the end, Matty, you understand?' Her voice sounded calm and reasonable now but belied the look on her face. 'You've been able to talk me around so far, but not any more. As for your dad . . .' She swept the things up from the table before ending, 'Just think of something to say to him when he sees his slippers, and hears that his coupon hasn't gone off.'

During this, Matty and Joe had been standing in the shadow of the scullery door, and Mrs

24

Doolin had been so incensed at the tribulation that had fallen on her through the presence of the dog in the house that she hadn't taken in her son's condition, but now, as she turned from the table, Matty came slowly into the kitchen, and she almost dropped the things from her arms as she exclaimed on a high note, 'Your coat! What's this now? Look at you . . . That's your new coat. Oh!' She closed her eyes and her head once again wagged in a wild movement as she ended, 'This is beyond a joke.'

'It . . . it wasn't his fault, Mrs Doolin. He . . .'

'You be quiet, Joe Darling. Matty's big enough to explain for himself. Now out with it.'

Matty went slowly towards his mother, and stood looking into her face. He supposed it was a bonny face but at the moment it was dark with temper. He liked his mother; he knew he was close to her and this made her happy, but lately he felt that it wasn't altogether a good thing, and sometimes he had a sort of guilty feeling when he wanted to get away from her. He said now, as if speaking to an equal, 'I've no need to tell you, you can see what happened. I've had a fight.'

He could see that his mother was taken aback by his direct approach. She would likely tell his father later that he was beyond coping with, but now she said, 'Get it off.' She made an impatient grab at the coat. 'Fighting at your age.'

'Well, Bill Cooper took the micky out of me about me name, and Joe's.'

'I'd have thought you'd have been past that, fighting about your name. There was a rhyme when I was a bairn and it still holds good:

25

> Sticks and stones will break me bones,
> But calling will not hurt me.

Get your old coat on,' she added, 'and I'll fix this when your dad's in bed, because if he sees it it'll be more than sticks and stones you'll get, it'll be the back of his hand.'

'Let him try it.' Matty turned away, his head wagging.

'Now, now, now,' Mrs Doolin admonished in a different tone, a stern, brook-no-back-chat tone. 'We'll have none of that. As long as you're here you'll do as your father says. You understand? And if I was you, instead of talking big I would start a long farewell to that thing there.' She pointed disdainfully down at Nelson. 'Because it's going. Whether you take it or I do, it's going. No wonder its last owners threw it out. Likely they were all driven mad and taken to the asylum.'

As Mrs Doolin left the room the two boys looked at each other. Then Matty, dropping slowly down on to the hearth rug, put his hand on Nelson's head, and as the dog nuzzled against him there came into his body a feeling so sad, so painful, that he understood in this moment why girls and women cried.

'What you goin' to do?' Joe pushed his face close to Matty's, and Matty, shaking his head, made no answer.

'I say, what about us going round houses like, and askin' them if they want a dog?' With this inspiration Joe's eyes widened, and, as Matty looked at him he didn't say 'Aw, don't be daft,' for he realized that Joe had thought of something. It was true it would still mean that he would lose Nelson, but it wouldn't be as final as if

26

he were put to sleep. And there was bound to be somebody somewhere like himself who loved animals. On average, there was just bound to be. It was finding them. Well, he'd have a try. His face lightened a little as he whispered, 'Good idea.'

Joe squared his narrow shoulders, pursed his lips into a whistle, then, bending down to Matty, hissed, 'Can you put the telly on?'

Matty wriggled forward and turned on the television; then flopping down again, he pulled Nelson across his knees and kept up a scratching movement with his fingers behind the dog's ear, while Joe, at the other end of Nelson, scratched his rump. And Nelson wondered why life could not be like this all the time.

It was half-an-hour later and the boys were still sitting on the hearth rug in the kitchen when Mr Doolin arrived home. His approach had been heralded with the yard door banging, then the kitchen door banging, followed by a pair of heavy boots, one after the other being thrown onto the stone floor of the scullery. And now his voice was calling, 'Where's me slippers?'

At this point Mrs Doolin entered the kitchen from the hallway, carrying in her hand a pair of tartan patterned cloth slippers. It was significant that she held them almost at arm's length from her, and more significant still that she cast a glance towards Matty as she crossed the room. And the glance brought Matty's head hanging. It also tightened his hold on Nelson.

The television cut off the muted conversation coming from the scullery, and Matty, still keeping his hold on Nelson, reached out and turned down the volume. But even now the conversation was no more audible, and Matty and Joe exchanged glances, until, following a brief silence, Mr Doolin's voice, loud now, came to them, crying, 'Well! This is the finish. It'll go, an' I'll see that he stumps up out of his pocket money and gets me a new pair of slippers.'

The injustice of this last remark brought Matty's eyes wide. Those particular slippers had been worn out years ago.

But now Mr Doolin was coming into the kitchen. He was a thick-set man, of medium height, and his hair was grey and strong looking, as was his face. Stubborn would be a better descriptive word here, for his lower jaw was squarish, and his nose blunt. But his mouth, when not pursed in some reprimand or dogmatic argument, looked kindly, as did his eyes.

'Well, me lad, what's this I'm hearin'?' Mr Doolin took his seat at the table and drank from a cup of tea which was already awaiting him, before slanting his glance towards Matty, adding, 'Well, what have you to say?'

Matty didn't know whether his father was alluding to his fighting or to Nelson, so he said, 'Nothing; me mam's told it to you all.'

'Now, now! I'm having none of your lip.'

'I'm not giving you any lip.' Matty's hand nervously stroked the dog's head, while Nelson cast a baneful glance up at the man sitting at the table. And the dog actually shrank closer to Matty as the finger came thrusting down towards him and Mr Doolin's deep voice cried, with finality, 'It's the end. It's gone past enough. He's going.'

Yet as awful as the final verdict was it wasn't delivered in the manner that Matty had expected, and he looked slowly sideways up at his father, and as he did so he realized that his father was in a good mood.

Mrs Doolin's voice broke Matty's concentrated stare as she said, 'Come on, get up out of that and have your tea . . . Come on, Joe.'

'Oh, thanks, Mrs Doolin.' Joe's smile was spread from ear to ear. He looked up at Matty's mam as if he was surprised at the invitation.

As Mrs Doolin placed plates of egg and chips before the boys, and one, to which was added a thick steak, in front of her husband, Matty's suspicion that his father was in a good mood was more than proved, for Mr Doolin, with a wry smile on his face, now bent his body towards Joe and asked in a confidential tone, 'How would you like to come here as a lodger?'

Under the circumstances the question might have appeared tactless, as this was Joe's third tea visit in a week, but Matty knew that had his father been really annoyed at Joe's presence he would have remained sullenly quiet until the boy had gone, and then let off steam.

Matty, forgetting for the moment the ominous fate that hung over Nelson, grinned at his pal, as Joe, not to be put out by any unsubtle jibes, jerked his head at his host and replied brightly, 'Oh, I'd like that fine, Mr Doolin.'

'You would?'

'Aye, I would fine.'

'And why?' Mr Doolin enquired, although he was asking what he well knew.

'Aw, well, 'cos Matty's mam's a grand cook an' she keeps everything nice like.'

Mr Doolin shook his head, this time in approval, and, looking to where his wife was seating herself at the other end of the table, he said, 'Well, what do you think of that, eh?'

'I think Joe's full of blarney.' Mrs Doolin's

voice sounded prim but she looked kindly towards the small boy. Then, her voice still holding the prim note, she said quickly, 'Get on with your teas; everything will be clay cold.'

The boys needed no second bidding. And it was such a good substantial tea, and the atmosphere was so genial, which under the circumstances appeared strange to Matty, that he would have felt totally happy at the moment if it hadn't been for the warm body pressed against his legs patiently waiting for that last tit-bit from his plate.

It wasn't until the meal was almost finished that the atmosphere changed. It was brought about quite suddenly as Joe, still aiming to be gallant, looked at Mrs Doolin and said, 'You'll have to give us some lessons in cookery afore we go to camp, Mrs Doolin.'

'What's this?' Mrs Doolin put down her knife and fork, then, turning on Matty, cried, 'Now, our Matty, I told you that was finished.'

'Aw, Mam.' Matty lowered his head.

'Don't aw Mam me. You said you wouldn't go with the school camp.'

'And I'm not.'

'Well then, don't let's bring all that up again. You're not going camping on your own. Now we've had enough for one day since you've come in. I told you the only way you could go was if you went with the school camp, or the youth club, and have someone with sense to see to things. And that's that.'

'But, Mam! I'm fifteen and if I haven't got sense now, I . . .'

'Now look here, Matty, you be quiet. I'm having no more of it. I'm telling you.' His mother's finger was wagging in his face, and

Matty looked away from it towards his father. And now his father said, 'Your mother's right. You can go campin' if you've got somebody to supervise things, but not on those fells by yourself.'

'But I'll not be by myself; there's Joe here' – Matty thumbed towards his friend – 'and Willie Styles. I've told you, Willie's been camping on his own afore.'

'Not miles away in the Lake District on those lonely fells. And Willie Styles hasn't the sense he was born with, he's nothing but talk. Oh, I wish you hadn't seen those fells; you've never been the same since.'

'Your mother's right,' put in Mr Doolin harshly. 'Since Jim Tollet took us for that ride that Sunday you've never been the same, and I say with her again, there's no camping on your own. You've just got to look at the papers and see what happens to youngsters when they go acting like men, and nobody to say them nay ... Get stuck up on a mountain and break their necks tryin' to get down, and endanger other folks in helpin' them.'

'Aw, Dad.' Matty made a deep obeisance with his head, and the action seemed to infuriate Mr Doolin, for he thrust out his arm and grabbed his son. And when Matty's body tensed and his face darkened Mrs Doolin, slapping at her husband's arm, cried, 'That's enough of that. It doesn't warrant a row.' Again she slapped at her husband's arm, harder this time, and Mr Doolin, drawing in a deep breath, released his hold, saying, 'You'll go too far one of these days, me lad.'

It was at this point that a voice from the yard came to them, calling, 'Matty, Matty, are you there?'

31

'That's Willie,' put in Joe in a very small voice, looking towards Matty. But before Matty could reply or move towards the scullery, his mother exclaimed, 'Oh, is it? Well, I'll see Mr Willie. We might as well get this cleared up once an' for all.'

'Aw, Mam, leave it be; I'll tell him.' Matty's voice was trembling slightly.

'I've told you to tell him afore, me lad, and if you'd done so he wouldn't be round here the night . . . not on his club night, and we wouldn't have had these ructions.'

On this, Mrs Doolin marched to the door, but the next moment returned to the kitchen, standing aside to allow Willie Styles to enter the room . . .

Willie was Matty's senior by three months. He was as tall as Matty but without his sturdiness, being very thin with a long, lugubrious face. Nothing about Willie inspired confidence, or gave evidence of stability. He had the nervous habit of twitching his nose, very much like that of a rabbit. Moreover, when he got excited he stammered. Willie's manner and conversation were naturally funny, and he played on this.

'Evenin', Mr Doolin.' Willie nodded his long head at Matty's father, and did not seem in the least disconcerted when Mr Doolin ignored the greeting.

'Hello, there, Joe.' Willie nodded to Joe, and Joe, grinning, nodded back.

'Now you can stop all this small chit-chat, Willie,' said Mrs Doolin. 'Up to a few weeks ago we never saw hilt or hare of you on a Tuesday or Friday, for you were too busy with the lads in the club practising your guitars, and it's now Friday night, so what are you after?'

'Oh, nowt . . . nothing, Mrs Doolin. I just

32

wanted a word with Matty.' He cast his eyes in Matty's direction and kept them there while he said, 'To tell him I've got me tent.'

Mrs Doolin pressed her lips together, and, lowering her head, wagged it slowly before saying, 'What did I tell you, our Matty? I told you to tell Willie there was no camping holiday for you, not just the three of you.' She raised her head as she added, 'After the schemozzle in the house last Saturday I'd have thought you would have had the sense to finish it.'

'Aw.' Willie was moving from one leg to the other now. 'Well, Mrs Doolin, he's never seen me since. He . . . he would have told me else.'

'Be quiet, Willie, and don't be so silly. In the same school and not seeing each other! Walking up the road together for years and not seeing each other . . .! Oh boy.' She flicked her hand at him impatiently, and he came back at her with a disarming smile, saying quietly, 'We . . . ell, Mrs Doolin, I've been off bad . . . cold, you know.'

There was a pause before Mrs Doolin asked, 'All the week?'

'Aw well, no. Just since Wednesday.'

'Well then, he had plenty of time to tell you, Willie.' She nodded towards Matty. 'But if he didn't, I'm tellin' you now. He's going on no camping holiday. Is that final? And nothing you can say will make me change me mind. Do you get that?'

Willie did not answer, and there was silence in the room now, and Mrs Doolin looked from him to Joe, who stood just to the side of him. Then she lifted her eyes to her son, and their glances held before her eyes dropped to Nelson, where the dog was squatting peacefully on the mat, and she exclaimed impatiently, 'With one thing and another I'm about distracted. Go on, get yourself

33

out.' She was addressing Matty now. 'And take that animal with you. And remember what I told you about him an' all. If you don't do it I will. Or,' she added, 'your dad will.'

Matty's gaze dropped slowly away from his mother's, and, stooping, he tugged Nelson gently to his feet. The other boys made for the door, and Willie, endeavouring to be polite to the last, said, 'Good-night, Mr Doolin; and you too Mrs Doolin. Good-night.'

'Good-night.' Mr Doolin's reply sounded flat, while Mrs Doolin, with a helpless air, said, 'Aw, good-night, Willie.'

'Thank you for the tea, Mrs Doolin; it was grand. Thanks a lot.' It was Joe now, addressing her, and she half-smiled at him as she said, 'That's all right, Joe.'

The three boys were going into the yard when Matty suddenly stopped and handed the dog to Joe, saying quietly, 'Take him down the yard, will you; I won't be a minute.' Then he went back into the kitchen, and there interrupted a muttered conversation that was passing between his parents. He stood staring at them until his father, with his usual form of enquiry, said, 'Well?'

Matty held them both a moment longer in his glance before he asked stiffly, 'You really mean it, that you won't let me go campin'?' He watched his mother close her eyes before saying, 'I thought you'd have sense to know we've had it all out. Do I have to repeat it again? You're not going camping on the fells with those two alone. With a crowd, yes, but not just by yourselves. They haven't got two pennorth of gumption atween them. Anything could happen.'

'Is that enough for you?' asked his father menacingly.

Matty now wetted his lips; then swallowed before he said, 'And you really mean that I've got to get rid of Nelson, that . . . that he's got to go some place the morrow?'

His mother looked at his father, then wearily back to him as she said slowly, 'Boy, I've told you. It isn't only that he tears up things, it's his howling. From the minute you leave the house that animal howls to high heaven. The street is raised; people are complaining.'

Again the three of them stood looking at each other. Then, his head drooping, Matty half turned away, only to pause. Bringing his head up again, he gazed deliberately at his father now and said, 'I'm on sixteen and I can't go campin', and I'm not allowed to keep me dog, so don't you be surprised if I want to do something else . . . like jumping a boat, say.'

'You young . . .!' His father's advancing figure and his voice were checked by his mother crying, 'Now that's enough . . . Go and get yourself out, boy.'

Matty was trembling when, with Nelson on a lead now, he followed his pals out of the back-yard door, and he didn't know whether it was with indignation at being treated like a small boy, or at Nelson's coming fate, or because he had dared to stand up to his father. Perhaps it was a little of all three.

2

The boys walked slowly, dolefully discussing the failure of their plans for the summer holidays. At least Willie and Joe made their disappointment verbal, but Matty's disappointment could find no outlet in words, because it probed beyond the fact that he was being done out of a holiday to the wider issue of being thought incapable of taking care of himself. Then there was Nelson. Nelson's plight was of more importance at the moment than the holiday or anything else. As the other two boys chatted, his thoughts were dwelling on Joe's proposal and he said now, 'We could start up White Leas way.'

'White Leas?' repeated Willie. 'What are we going to do up White Leas way?'

'Joe here thought that somebody might take Nelson.'

'Aye, I did.' Joe nodded brightly. 'It would be better than have him gassed the morrow.'

'He'll not be gassed.' Matty turned on his pal. 'Don't say that. They stick a needle in them and put them to sleep; they're not gassed.'

'All right, all right. Eeh! You are in a tear. I only said . . .'

'I know what you said.'

'You mean,' said Willie, bending in front of

Matty to look at Joe now, 'you mean, go round the doors and ask?'

'Yes,' said Joe.

'Good idea,' said Willie. 'But why White Leas? Why not go down Westoe?'

'Use your napper,' said Matty. 'Westoe! Who'd take a stray dog down Westoe? They're snooty down there; more likely set their dogs on you if you went to a gate. No, we're going up White Leas.'

'Aye,' said Joe, 'Matty is right. White Leas is best.'

The first door they went to was painted yellow and had a bell, which Joe took upon himself to ring, his finger pressed tightly on it for some seconds. They were all in different states of nervousness as they waited, but when after some minutes there was no response to their ringing, it was evident there was no one at home.

'We'll knock next door,' said Willie.

'No,' said Matty, pulling Nelson on to the pavement again.

'Why for not?' asked Joe.

'Well, it looks scruffy,' said Matty. His eyes were skimming over the doors as he spoke. Then he pointed. 'There's a nice one. It's just been varnished and the house has got nice windows, nice curtains.'

Again Joe rang a doorbell, and this time it was opened almost immediately by a little girl of about eight. 'What do you want?' she said, without any preamble.

Joe and Willie remained silent, their gaze on Matty now, as he swallowed deeply before saying, 'Is your ma in? Will you ask her if she wants a dog?'

'A dog?' The little girl's voice was high and

excited, and, looking at Nelson, she added, 'Him!'

'Aye. He's a good dog,' said Matty, 'friendly like.'

'Ma!' The little girl was running back up the passage. They heard her voice gabbling to someone beyond the closed door, then a woman made her appearance. She was big and fat and seemed to fill the space between the walls, and she cried at them, 'A dog! A dog, is it? Now get yerselves away afore I bite yer. Go on with you.'

The next minute they were looking at the closed door. When they were on the pavement once more they were silent, until Willie, chuckling slowly, said, 'Did you hear what she said? She said, "afore I bite yer." It's funny, isn't it, trying to get her to take a dog, and her tellin' us she'll bite us, see?'

'Aye, it is funny.' Joe was laughing with Willie now. But Matty wasn't laughing. He felt awful, he felt as if the woman had slapped him in the face. He had a feeling of being humiliated somehow, and at this moment his thoughts returned to his mother and he felt bitter against her. All this was happening to him because she wouldn't let him keep Nelson.

At another house a man answered the door. He was a thin oldish man, and they knew he was a pitman by the blue marks on his face and arms, the insignia of hewing coal. Although his refusal was firm, his voice was kindly and went some ways towards soothing Matty's feelings. 'No, lad,' he said. 'We don't want a dog. We've had enough trouble with animals and bairns over the years, and now the wife's past bothering. You know what I mean; she wants to get out a bit, and you can't leave an animal tied up for hours on end.' He looked at Matty knowingly and added, 'Your mother won't let you keep him?'

Matty nodded his head.

'Well, I'm sorry for you, lad, and I don't doubt your trek is goin' to be a hard one, 'cos as soon as the licence is due they push them out. Not all, oh no, not all. There's some folks love their dogs but there are others who are not fit to keep rats. Still, I wish you luck, lad.'

'Thanks,' said Matty.

The next door they visited was painted blue, and as they rang the bell there came the sound of raised voices, and Willie, bending towards Matty, whispered, 'They're having a row.'

Matty had realized this and was just about to turn away when the door was wrenched open and they were faced by a young woman glowing with temper. 'What do you want?'

Matty stared up at her but said nothing. He knew that in this particular case the offering of a dog would only be adding fuel to the fire. But Joe didn't think along these lines, for, looking up at the woman and giving her his brightest smile, he said, 'Would you like a dog, missus?'

'You cheeky monkey!' A very large hand came out, and the next minute Joe found himself sitting on the concrete looking at the bottom of a closed door, while Willie hung over the railings laughing at the top of his lungs, and Matty, his head bowed, found it almost impossible not to bellow with him, and, try as he might, he couldn't keep his face straight as he pulled Joe to his feet.

Their visits to the last three houses had been observed by a boy of about ten years old. He had been pushing a bike along the other side of the street. One tyre of the bike was quite flat, making it evident why he was walking. And now he

39

turned the bike in the direction of the boys, and when he came up to them, he said, 'You trying to get rid of your dog?'

'Yes,' said Matty. 'Do you know anybody who wants one?'

'I do.' The boy was looking at Nelson, and they all looked at the boy, and Joe and Willie now gabbled together, 'Great! Great! He's yours, isn't he, Matty? You can have him.'

'Wait a minute. Where do you live?' asked Matty.

'Up the close,' said the boy, still gazing at Nelson. 'Second turning from here.'

'Are you the only one?' said Matty.

'No.' The boy looked up at him now. 'I've a sister but she's mad for a dog an' all. We've always wanted a dog, and me ma promised we could have one sometime.'

'We'll go and see your ma,' said Matty.

Excited now, and headed by the boy, they made their way to No. 4 The Close, only to find that the boy's mother was not at home. But his sister was.

'Look, Ann!' the boy cried. 'These lads don't want their dog; they say we can have him.' The girl was apparently a little younger than the boy, and though she looked at Nelson with open affection she did not show as much enthusiasm as her brother about accepting him. 'Better wait till me ma comes in,' she said.

'Oh, it's all right,' said the boy. 'You know she said last week that we could have one, didn't she?'

'Yes.' The girl nodded. 'Yes, she did.' She brightened and, dropping on to her knees, she looked into Nelson's face, and was captivated immediately when he put out his tongue and gen-

40

tly licked her. Looking up at Matty, she said, 'Oh, he's lovely. Why do you want to get rid of him?'

Staring down into the upturned face, the truth stopped between Matty's teeth. If he told the real reason that would be the finish of Nelson. As he groped for a substitute reason, Willie came to the rescue by exclaiming loudly, 'They're moving.' And this was endorsed by Joe saying, 'Aye. Aye, they're going to Sea Houses.' He laughed at his own ingeniousness. He had once been to Sea Houses and would have liked to stay there, and now he was making Matty move there. He returned Matty's wide stare and only prevented himself from winking.

'What time will your mother be back?' asked Matty now. And the girl answered, 'Oh, she'll likely be late; she's gone to me Aunt Mary's.'

Matty thought for a moment; then said, 'We'll leave him with you, and I'll tell you where I live so . . . so if it isn't all right with her you can let me know.'

'Yes. Yes, that'll be fine,' said the boy eagerly.

'Does he eat a lot?' asked the girl.

'No,' Matty lied. 'Just what you can give him . . . Here.' Abruptly he handed her Nelson's lead, and, turning quickly, he marched out of the yard.

When Joe and Willie caught up with him, Joe said, 'You never said good-bye to him; we did. He licked us all over.'

'Shut your trap. You talk too much.' Matty strode ahead, the other two having to jump a step every now and again to keep up with him.

'He'll be all right,' said Willie after a time. 'Anyway, you know he's alive an' you know where he is and you can go on the sly now and again and have a look at him.'

As they neared home Joe said, 'What are we

41

going to do about the camping?' and he actually started as Matty turned on him and bawled, 'You heard me mam and dad, didn't you? Wasn't that final enough?'

'Coo!' said Joe. 'I don't know why I put up with you.'

'Well, you don't have to,' said Matty, thrusting his face down to his pal. 'There's no pressure from this side. And that goes for you too.' And he turned his white face towards Willie, before marching off and leaving the boys open-mouthed, gazing after him.

Over the past hour Mrs Doolin had tried to hide her relief. She felt happy. Matty was a good boy; he had done as he was told and got rid of the pest. She showed her appreciation by piling his plate high at supper time with cold pie and pickles. But her disappointment was evident when Matty, pushing the meal away, muttered, 'I'm not hungry.'

'Now, you eat your supper,' she said. 'And be sensible. Now go on; there's a good lad.'

'Get it down you,' said his father. 'There's never any use worryin' over spilt milk. What's done's done.'

'If you don't mind,' said Matty rising from the table, 'I'll go up; I'm a bit tired.'

Mrs Doolin's voice cut off the reply his father was about to make. 'All right. Do that,' she said.

It was as Matty reached the passage that the front-door bell rang, and his mother, rising from the table, said, 'You go on; I'll see who it is.'

Matty was halfway up the stairs when his mother opened the door, and he stopped dead as a voice demanded, 'Is this yours?' He turned to see a woman standing on the step holding Nelson by

42

his lead. Slowly now he descended the stairs as the woman went on, 'Foisting him off on to a pair of bairns! Well, you can take him to Sea Houses with you. When I get a dog for them it won't be an old blind one like this, with a howl like a banshee. Here, take him, and good-night to you.'

Nelson was now bounding round Matty's knees, and Mrs Doolin, who hadn't had a chance to open her mouth, stood helplessly with the door in her hand. Then, closing it slowly and still looking a bit dazed, she said, 'Well that's settled that. You'll take him down to the P.D.S.A. tomorrow mornin'. You've tried and you've failed, so that's all there is to it. Put him in the shed. Go on.'

When he led Nelson through the kitchen his father just gazed at him and the dog, and for once made no comment. And as he went out into the back-yard his mother, seeming to have regained her wits, cried, 'What's this about Sea Houses? What did she mean?'

When Matty put Nelson in the shed he bent his head down and the dog licked him furiously. But when Matty closed the door on him Nelson lamented this fresh separation in the only way he knew how. He howled.

'Nice thing, isn't it? Nice thing,' his mother greeted him when he entered the kitchen. 'The neighbourhood raised at this time of night. Well, you know what you've got to do. Go on up.' She nodded her head towards the stairs. 'And remember, you'll have to face up to worse than this afore you die.'

The following morning Matty, in a last desperate effort to keep Nelson, reasoned that if he made himself scarce straight after breakfast and stayed out all day his mother couldn't do much

43

about it, for she herself would never take the dog to the P.D.S.A., nor, he imagined, would his father.

So after he returned from his paper round, and after a silent meal, he went into the scullery, picked up his coat and slipped away.

Matty did not go and call for either Joe or Willie, for he knew that today he would be very bad company and would probably only snap at his pals, so he decided to go down to the sands. Later, he would buy himself some fish and chips for his dinner, after which he would spend the afternoon in the pictures. That would take care of most of the day.

Besides the half-crown his father left for him every Friday night on the mantelpiece, he had in his pocket his wages from his paper round. These he generally handed over to his mother immediately after breakfast, when she would give him back five shillings; the rest she put away for him, for, as she said, he would need it on a 'rainy day'. Matty considered, metaphorically speaking, he'd had lots of rainy days, but his mother had never been induced to break into his little hoard, not even when he had pleaded with her. Well, anyway, seven and sixpence of the money in his pocket was his, and this would see him through . . .

Matty kept strictly to his plan. He went to the sands, had fish and chips, then on to the pictures. When he came out of the pictures at half-past four he told himself that if he took his time walking home he should get in just after five.

Whilst on his way home, he hoped his dad wouldn't grab at him for this always made him want to hit out; and he hoped Nelson hadn't howled too much; but mostly he hoped that his mother wasn't wild. Altogether he felt highly nervous, and not a little fearful.

Brinkburn Street was usually quiet at the week-end. There was less coming and going; people hadn't to go to work. On a Saturday afternoon some of the women went shopping and took the children with them, and the men, those who liked cricket, went to the match. Others sat indoors looking at the telly; anyway, Saturday afternoon and Sunday brought a change to the street, but now, as Matty went past the bottom of the street on his way to the back lane he was brought to an abrupt halt, for there, up at the top end, near where he lived, stood small groups of adults, surrounded by a large number of children, and their attention was centred on two men, one of whom – whose voice Matty recognized with dismay – was his father. A wave of shame enveloped him. His dad rowing in the street. Was he drunk? His father never got drunk; their family was respectable. His father like a drink but he never stayed late in the pubs and then came rolling home to fight. His mam would never have stood that. His mam laid great stock on their being considered respectable.

Slowly and unnoticed, Matty walked up the street; unnoticed, that was, until he came to the outskirts of the crowd. Then a woman, turning and looking at him, exclaimed, 'Aw, Matty, lad.' There was such commiseration in the woman's tone that Matty's heart gave a painful jerk. Something had happened to his mam? Careless of whom he was pushing, he went through the people, until he came to the clear space where stood his father, facing Mr Tollet, and his father was shouting, 'Don't tell me you were only doing twenty. Sixty more like it. You should be had up.'

'Look, man,' said Mr Tollet in a calming tone. 'I haven't killed anybody; it was just the dog. An' if you had looked after it it wouldn't have been running wild, would it?'

Mr Doolin, about to retort, became aware of Matty standing at his side, and, his aggressive manner and voice changing, he appeared and sounded flustered as he said, 'Aw, lad, there you are then. Well, look. Come on ... come on indoors.' He made the unusual gesture of putting his arm around his son's shoulders and leading him through the crowd towards the open front door, which he shut forcibly behind them with a thrust of his foot. Then, still keeping his hold on Matty, he led him into the kitchen, where Mrs Doolin sat, her elbows on the table, her face buried in her hands.

On their entry, Mrs Doolin raised her tear-stained face to her son and brokenly said, 'Oh, Matty.'

Matty made no reply, not even to ask the obvious question, for he knew by the dreadful dead weight inside him that something irrevocable had happened to Nelson.

'I ... I didn't mean it, Matty, not like that I didn't. Believe me I didn't.'

'Now, now, Jean.' Mr Doolin went towards his wife. 'Give over, it wasn't your fault. It was that damned maniac racing round the corner.'

'It was ... it was, Matty.' Mrs Doolin put her hand out towards Matty now. 'It was my fault.'

Ignoring her pleading gesture, Matty asked, in a voice that didn't sound like his own, even to himself, 'Where is he?'

'He's in the shed, lad.' It was his father speaking. 'He'll likely be gone by now. He was in a bad way.'

On these words Matty seemed to come to life, and he cried, 'He's not dead then?'

'Now don't excite yourself.' Mr Doolin himself preceded Matty through the scullery. 'He could be; he was as near enough to it as makes no odds a few minutes ago.'

Matty, scrambling now, pushed past his father, ran down the yard and pulled open the shed door, there to see a pitiful sight. Nelson lay on his side, his blood-soaked hindquarters showing where the car had hit him. His eyes were closed and he appeared dead, but as Matty, dropping slowly to his knees, laid a trembling hand on his head, the dog gave a slight shiver and opened his eyes. Both eyes were glazed, his good eye looking almost as opaque as the one with the cataract on it.

When Nelson, making one more valiant effort, licked weakly at Matty's hand, Matty, throwing himself almost flat on the ground, laid his face near the dog's. But still he neither spoke nor made a sound, not even when his father said, 'Don't get too near him like that, lad. You don't know what you'll catch.'

As Matty, his body seeming to swell with the queer pain that was filling him, held Nelson's head between his hands, the dog slowly closed his eyes, and his tongue becoming limp where its tip touched Matty's thumb, it died as it would have wished, in the hands of the kindest of its many masters.

When Matty, with his head sunk on his chest, continued kneeling by the dog, his father said, 'Well, it's over. He couldn't have been in much pain, he'd be numb. It affects you like that when the legs are smashed. Come on.' And he thrust his hand, not ungently, under Matty's arm, and

47

pulled him to his feet, adding under his breath, 'Your mam's in a state; she's blaming herself. Now don't you make it worse for her . . . you understand?'

Matty pulled himself from his father's hold and went slowly up the yard and into the kitchen, there to be met by his mother. She was still crying, and after staring at him for a moment she shook her head as she said again, 'Oh, I'm sorry, I am that. I wouldn't have had it happen like this for the world. Only I was so vexed at you running off this morning, and then you not coming in to your dinner, and him howlin' all the time, and her next door sending Mr Watson in to say we'd have to do something about it, and you still not coming home. I . . . I felt so vexed and upset, so . . . so I pushed him out into the back lane. I know I shouldn't have done it, but as I said I was vexed. But I wouldn't for the world it had happened like . . . like this. Believe me, Matty.'

Mrs Doolin paused and waited for Matty to say something. But he could say nothing that would relieve her self-reproach. His head bowed once again, he was making his way towards the room door when she put her hand out tentatively towards him. She did not touch him but she said brokenly, 'Won't . . . won't you stay and have your tea? It's fish.'

It was too much. Nelson, unusually perhaps for a dog, had been very partial to fish. Turning swiftly from her, Matty went into the hall, and, taking the stairs two at a time, he reached his room and banged the door after him. Then flinging himself on to his bed, he grabbed up fistfuls of pillow; and when he dropped his face onto his hands he saw on the black screen of his mind the picture of Nelson dashing down the back lane, after his mam had pushed him out, looking first one way and then the other before deciding that he would find his master in the front street. He could see him rushing headlong into the car, and for a moment he actually felt the impact, and his own legs jerked in sympathetic reaction.

As the burning in his eyes intensified and his throat swelled to bursting point, the bedroom door was thrust open and his father stalked in. Matty felt him standing over him. And now his voice beat down on him, saying, 'Now look here. Your mother's been through enough this afternoon without you makin' it worse for her. She was nearly out of her mind when I came in. She carried that dog up the road herself, wouldn't let anybody touch it. She's taken all the blame to herself when it's you who are to blame. For if you had done what you were told the animal would have died peacefully. But no . . . no, you think you're right. You're always right, aren't you? So you took yourself out on a jaunt for the day, not really carin' two hoots what happened to the . . .'

'I didn't take meself out on a jaunt. I didn't.' Matty swung round on his elbow as he bawled back at his father. But Mr Doolin did not raise his hand or cry at him, 'Now look here, me lad, I'm havin' none of your cheek,' because he saw his son was crying. He watched the slow painful tears rolling down Matty's face before, his own head drooping, he turned slowly away and went quietly out of the room.

On Monday, Matty played truant from school, and his mother got to know for the simple reason that Joe came round to see if his pal was ill. Matty intended to make no secret of his default, for he did not return home until six o'clock, when

49

his mother, more worried than ever, reproached him, but quietly, saying, 'You shouldn't have done it, Matty. And you so near finishing school. It'll be a black mark against you.'

The expression on Matty's face told her what he thought about black marks, and it aroused his father to shout, 'Now look here, me lad. Saturday's over and done with, and the quicker you forget it the better it'll be for you, because you're not going to upset the house and all in it on account of a dog.'

But Mr Doolin found he couldn't keep upbraiding someone who didn't answer.

On Tuesday, Matty went to school and at nine-thirty, accompanied by Mr Borley, he stood before the headmaster, who first of all went into the incident of Friday night; then he said he understood that Matty had played truant yesterday and openly admitted it this morning. What had he to say about all this?

Matty's answer was, 'Nothing, sir.'

The headmaster then dismissed Mr Borley from the study, much to that gentleman's annoyance, and endeavoured to get beneath the façade of the big, reticent boy. But after twenty minutes of his precious time, the headmaster realized, as he had done so many times before, that the breaking down of walls with which boys at times surrounded themselves demanded more than minutes of time to accomplish. He also realized, as he had done before, that men like Mr Borley were an obstacle to progress when dealing with the Matty Doolins of this world.

When the headmaster dismissed Matty it was with a strong reprimand, and without caning.

It was during the last week at school that Matty

50

experienced another form of hurt. This was caused by the blatant desertion of Joe and Willie. This desertion was so obvious that it brought jibes from Bill Cooper, such as: 'So darling Joe has walked out on you.' And, 'Willie Styles doesn't want to go about with a bigger nit-wit than himself.'

It further troubled Matty at this stage that he didn't want to pounce on Bill Cooper, and he was surprised when he said to himself, 'Let him talk. He keeps acting like a bairn.' Following this thought Matty had felt a kind of superior feeling, as if he were years older than Bill Cooper. But whereas he could dismiss what Bill Cooper said, he could not dismiss the feeling created by the desertion of his pals. They were both, he knew, excited about going into the docks and the Technical School. Yet, he reasoned, this shouldn't make them avoid him; they had never done such a thing before. Joe, in particular, had trailed him every free hour of the day right back as far as he could remember.

The memory of Nelson too had been with him every moment of the past week. For the first few days he had imagined, at odd times, that he saw the dog bounding around him. Then an odd thing began to happen. When he tried to visualize Nelson he couldn't get him into shape, not to look like Nelson. He'd see a little dog, or a sausagey dog, or a dog as big as a Great Dane. He would see all kinds of dogs, but not Nelson.

It was on the Wednesday night as he walked home alone from school that he thought: It's as me dad says, you can never trust anybody, not even yourself.

And it was in this frame of mind that Matty entered the house. As usual he came in through

51

the scullery and into the familiar kitchen. But now it was no longer familiar.

Matty stood gaping at the sight before him, for the whole kitchen was covered with camp equipment. There, taking up the space before the fire, stood a four-foot-high ridge tent. Between the sideboard and the table was stretched a sleeping bag, on top of which were neatly stacked three blankets, and an old eiderdown. This had evidently been sewn to form a bag. On the table was arrayed an enamel plate and mug, a knife, fork and spoon, an all-purpose billy, and a miniature Primus stove.

Matty just gaped from one thing to the other, and he wondered for a moment if he had come into the wrong house.

Then a suppressed giggle coming from the passage brought his head sharply round towards the partly open door, and the next moment it was thrust wide and Joe bounced into the kitchen, followed more slowly by Mrs Doolin.

'What do you think, Matty? Isn't it great?' Joe was hopping from one side to the other in his excitement.

'Aye.' The muscles of Matty's face were sagging so much that he didn't seem able to close his mouth. Now he looked straight at his mother, and although Mrs Doolin returned his look she did not speak. He watched her swallow twice before he moved swiftly towards her. But all he could say was, 'Oh, Mam.'

Mrs Doolin put out her hand and touched her son's face and asked softly, 'Are you pleased?'

'Pleased?' It was Matty's turn to swallow hard, and then he said in a rush, 'I don't know what to say, Mam, only you shouldn't have done it, not spent all this. I . . . I could have gone on

52

half of this stuff, but . . . but thanks, Mam. I know what it must have cost, an' I . . . I don't mean only in money. You understand? I mean for you to let me go campin'.'

'Well!' Mrs Doolin turned abruptly away, saying now with a slightly tart tone to her voice, 'It's what you wanted, isn't it?'

'Yes, yes, Mam, it is.'

'Well then, that's all right. Now let's get this stuff off the table and get the tea going; your dad will be in in no time.'

'Does he know, Mam?'

Mrs Doolin looked at Matty over her shoulder, her eyebrows slightly raised. 'Of course he knows. He went with me and Joe here.' She flung out her hand towards Joe who was still grinning widely. 'He went with us to pick the things. He seemed to know more about what was needed than any of us.'

Matty drew in a long breath, and let it out slowly before he said, 'That's good.' But as he looked down at the three blankets reposing on the sleeping bag, a section of his mind doubted whether his father did know very much about camping. How did he expect him to lug a tent, a sleeping bag and three blankets, as well as all the other paraphernalia, around on his back? And then there was that big eiderdown. That was likely his mam's idea. Altogether there was far too much stuff. But he would say nothing for a time. Oh no, he'd better say nothing that would upset either of them. He'd far rather set out with the whole caboodle and park half of it some place, then pick it up on their return. But all that could be arranged.

As the boys, their arms full of camping equipment, made towards the back door, Mrs Doolin exclaimed in a high tone, 'You're not putting that

53

stuff in the shed. You can put it in the front room for now; it'll get damp down there.'

On this, the boys exchanged amazed glances; then laughing, turned and carried the equipment into the front room. And as Matty laid his pile on the hearth rug he knew that he was actually taking part in another miracle, for the front room was his mother's pride and joy and was rarely used except at Christmas, or when special company came . . .

But it would appear that this was a day of miracles, because half-an-hour later, when his father came into the house, he brought with him a brown-paper parcel, and, throwing it nonchalantly on to the easy chair to the side of the fireplace, he looked from his wife's averted face to Joe's grinning countenance, and lastly he met the straight gaze of his son. Then rubbing his hand over his bristled chin, he exclaimed, 'Aye, well, you all look like a kitchen full of liver-fed cats.' Being Mr Doolin, he couldn't help adding, 'And that's a change, I'm sure.'

'Now come, sit yourselves down,' said Mrs Doolin, still without looking at her husband. And as Mr Doolin went to his seat, Matty, who had not moved his eyes from his father's face, said quietly, 'Thanks, Dad.'

'Aw!' Mr Doolin's response was immediate. 'So you've seen it all, have you?'

'Yes, Dad.'

'Well, what do you think?'

'Grand. Everything's grand; it couldn't be better.'

'Aye, well, although I say it meself I haven't forgotten what's needed to go campin'. Although mind' – he jabbed his finger towards his son – 'don't think we had that lot when we slept out. Aw, no. A ground sheet and a blanket was our lot, and frozen toes, and your eyelashes with icicles on them.'

'Well, those days are gone, and thank goodness. Sit up, Joe,' put in Mrs Doolin briskly.

'Thanks, Mrs Doolin. Aw, thanks.'

'By the way' – Mrs Doolin turned her gaze towards the armchair – 'what have you got in there?'

Mr Doolin now looked towards the parcel, and in a tone that suggested he had forgotten all about it, said, 'Oh, that ... Oh, aye. Well.' He cast a sidelong glance towards Matty now. 'You'd better open it and see, hadn't you?'

'Me, Dad?' Matty scraped his chair back from the table.

'Well, I'm sure your mother won't be wantin' them.'

Somewhat mystified, Matty picked up the parcel and, tearing off the brown paper, revealed a bright green canvas bucket, together with its matching basin. The first thought that came into his mind was, some more things to carry, but, glancing towards his father and seeing the warm pride in his mother's face brought there by his father's generosity, he rose to the occasion and exclaimed, 'Coo! Talk about doing things in style.' He held the bucket swinging by its rope handle. 'Look at this, Joe.' Again he paused and looked at his father and said, with sincerity, 'Thanks a lot, Dad,' for he realized that his father's gift put a final stamp on this day as a day of miracles.

'Aw, you shouldn't be thankin' me, it's your mother you should be thankin'. She put the idea into me head. Scared stiff you wouldn't keep your

55

neck clean. You know how to use the basin, don't you? Look.' Mr Doolin rose hastily from the table and, going to the fireplace, took up the poker, the tongs, and a long hearth brush, and criss-crossing them demonstrated as he exclaimed, 'Three sticks like that, you see. Good firm ones lashed together; then just hook your basin on it an' you're set up . . . hot and cold,' he added on a deep laugh.

'Will you sit down and get your tea! Everything will be ruined.'

When they were seated once more and were busy with their eating, there came a slight lull in the excited conversation. Then Matty, his mind still on the transporting of the growing camping equipment, looked at his mother and said, 'I'll have to dip into me savings, Mam, to get a big rucksack.'

'You've got your dad's old knapsack; isn't that good enough?'

'Oh, it won't hold half the stuff. I'll want something bigger so's I can put the tent roll on the top and get it on me back.'

'On your back!' Mrs Doolin's voice ended up in a high squeak. 'You don't think you're carrying that lot on your back, do you? It's going by train.'

'By train?'

'That's what I said, by train. Willie's dad, as you know, is on the railway and he's going to have everything sent on together.'

Matty was silent for a moment, and his face dropped into set lines as he said, 'But . . . but it'll mean us stopping in one place.'

'Yes . . . yes, I'm afraid it'll mean just that.' Mrs Doolin's manner was prim again. 'Mr Styles heard of a farm . . . and it's on the fells, so don't worry, miles from anywhere he assures me, and that should suit you, and he's written to the farmer and everything's settled . . . There's one thing you're not going to do, and that is jaunt around the countryside and me not knowin' where you are.'

'Your mother's right.' Mr Doolin was nodding stiffly at his son, but his tone on this occasion wasn't convincing.

In the silence that returned to the tea-table Matty put his left hand down by the side of his chair – it was an unconscious movement – and when his fingers found no answering touch the memory of Nelson returned to him, and he was swept with a feeling of remorse, and guilt. He had completely forgotten about Nelson during the last hour. He had no need to ask himself how this had come about; it was only too evident. His mother had achieved her purpose.

The knowledge that things could happen to you that could take away the feeling of loss wasn't pleasant knowledge, Matty decided, for he did not want to forget Nelson – ever.

3

In a state of high excitement they arrived at
Hexham. They were hot, thirsty, hungry and
tired, but so excited they weren't aware of their
discomfort.

'We're nearly there. Look, we're running in.'
Joe was bouncing up and down like a cork at the
corridor window, and Willie, leaning over him,
pushed his head out of the window, saying, 'It
seems years since we left Tyne Dock.'

Matty, no less excited, pulled their cases from
the rack. There were four cases, and the two
largest belonged to him and one of them was full
of food. That was his mother's doing. Aw well. He
smiled to himself, then shouted to his pals, 'Here
you! Get your stuff.'

Like jack-in-the-boxes, the boys bounced into
the carriage and grabbed up their luggage, and
before the train had pulled itself to a stop Willie
was on the platform and almost on his face as he
missed his footing.

Matty held Joe by the collar until the train was
absolutely still, and when they alighted Matty
went for Willie, saying, 'It would have served you
right if you'd landed up on the track. Now I've
told you, Willie.' He wagged his finger in the
taller boy's face. 'Any of your daft antics and we
break it up.'

'Aw, all right, Matty man, I just wanted to get off. I'm so hot I feel fried. I want a drink.' He looked around, and Matty said, 'You've got to get your things out of the van, we're not seeing to them. You can have a drink after, so come on.'

When finally their luggage stood in a pile outside the station, they looked about them. Where was Mr Walsh? What was he like? Would he have a car? A Land-Rover or a lorry? They didn't know. Mr Styles had said that Mr Walsh would know them by their number, and this Matty pointed out to Willie when he was once again on the point of leaving them to get a drink. 'Look,' he said, 'if he just sees two of us he won't think it's us, he'll think we're some other blokes going campin'.'

To this confusing but apparently, to Willie, lucid statement, he replied, 'But, Matty, man, I'm chokin'.'

'Well, you go on chokin'.' Matty nodded at him briskly. 'And when you peg out we'll bury you.' Again they were laughing, Willie included. He didn't mind if the joke was against himself. Matty was in fine form. Oh, they were going to have a spanking time . . . But if only he could have a drink.

Ten minutes later, all three were still standing outside the station. The cars had thinned out considerably, and so had the people, and what was very evident was that nobody was rushing round looking for three boys with camping equipment.

It was when they had been waiting for half-an-hour and Matty was really beginning to worry that a small dilapidated-looking lorry drew to a stop in front of them, and a man, getting down from the cab, surveyed them for a moment in silence. Then he said, 'Well, you've arrived then.'

'You Mr Walsh?' asked Matty.

'Yes, I'm Mr Walsh.'

'We've been waiting for half-an-hour.' Willie smiled as he gave Mr Walsh this information. And Mr Walsh, looking from the crown of Willie's damp hair to his dusty shoes, then up again, replied, 'In that case you've had plenty of time to cool down, haven't you? Well, what are you waiting for? Get your stuff on.'

He let down the back of the lorry and stood aside while they loaded their gear, and when it was all on, he commanded, 'Get yourselves up now.'

'We ridin' in the back?' This was the first time Joe had spoken, and Mr Walsh gave him the same treatment as he had given Willie; he let his eyes rove over him before he said, 'Yes, little 'un, you're riding in the back. Did you think you were going to travel underneath her?'

'Eeh! No.' Joe's face was one broad grin. 'I thought we'd go up front.'

'You did, did you?' Mr Walsh's thick eyebrows moved upwards. 'Well, one of the things we've got to learn in this life is that every day brings its disappointments. Up with you!' His hand came so quickly under Joe's buttocks and hoisted him so rapidly from the ground into the truck that Joe gasped with surprise as he fell forward among the baggage.

Neither Willie nor Matty needed to be told what to do. They pulled themselves up smartly into the lorry, and Mr Walsh, after clipping the back into place, looked into their wide-eyed, somewhat startled faces, and remarked caustically, 'If you want to arrive safely, keep your seats.'

Matty's eyes followed Mr Walsh as he went

60

round the lorry and into the cab. He hadn't met anyone like him before. He had heard the term 'Brook no nonsense', and that apparently described Mr Walsh. Yet he was nothing to look at. He wasn't as big as his dad, nor as broad. But his body looked hard and knotty. A dig in the ribs from Joe brought his head down to his pal's level.

'He's a funny bloke.' Joe screwed his face up. 'Keep your seats, he says, and there's no seats. Coo! I wouldn't like to get on the wrong side of him. Did you see the way he hoisted me up? Eeh! I felt like the man on the flying trapeze.'

Soon they were outside the town, and, whereas Mr Walsh's thirty miles an hour had appeared to them like sixty, they would have sworn his fifty miles an hour was nothing less than a hundred.

They passed places called Elrington, Langley, Staward, Allendale, and Whitfield. After the last place the truck turned off the main road, and now, although the speed lessened, they found the going much more uncomfortable. At one point, when Joe ended up across Matty's legs and Matty loosened his hold on the side of the lorry to steady him, he found himself in the midst of their shifting baggage. When they sorted themselves they were again laughing, but not so heartily now.

It was as they were going round a bend on a rough road that Matty, looking at Willie, saw his face stretch in amazement. Looking over the back of the truck, his own eyes stretched, for what had made Willie's face pale was the fact that from the edge of the narrow road the hillside dropped almost sheer down to a valley far below.

The truck was going down-hill now, bumping, jolting, its speed increasing as the road became smoother. For a minute they were carried from

61

the bright sunshine into the dimness of a piece of woodland. It surprised them, so that they all looked upwards. It was as if the lorry had run into a shed. The next minute they were out again into the sunshine, and a short while later the lorry stopped with a jerk, and they sat in their contorted positions speechless, looking about them.

'Well, enjoyed it?' Mr Walsh was gazing at them from the roadway.

They gave him no answer, and when he let down the back of the truck they descended like drunken men to the ground and stood gazing about them. To the left of them lay fields, all marked out by stone walls. To the right of them, beyond another field, stood a house. It was built of big blocks of stone, which in the bright sunshine appeared white, so white it didn't look real to the boys. And to the right of it again lay the actual farm, low buildings forming three sides of a square.

'Well now, there's your field.' Mr Walsh pointed to a gate just off the road. 'Come on, get your stuff in, and I'll tell you the rules.' He opened the gate for them and stood aside as they humped the cases, rucksacks and kitbags into the field. Then closing the gate, he walked quickly past them, saying, 'Bring what you can and follow me.'

Again they did as he bade them, but they couldn't keep up with him for their feet kept slipping into ruts in the uneven ground.

When he stopped, Matty was first to reach him and Mr Walsh stamped the ground, saying, 'I would pitch your tent here. It's level, and the view's good. Well now.' He looked from Willie to Joe as they came up, then let his gaze rest on Matty. 'You the eldest?'

'No.' Matty pointed to Willie. 'Willie's older than me.'

'Is he the boss of your outfit?'

'No. No, he isn't.' It was Joe's piping voice now. 'Matty here is.'

To this Willie amicably conceded. His long face grinning, he said, 'Aye, Matty's the boss.'

'Well,' said Mr Walsh, staring straight at Matty, 'I'll hold you responsible.'

'Eh?' Matty screwed up his face. 'Responsible for what?'

'For three things,' said Mr Walsh flatly. 'First of all, you keep the gates closed.'

'But the sheep are wandering all over the . . .'

Matty did not finish this remark because Mr Walsh put in quickly, 'Yes, the sheep are wandering all over the place. But it's not the sheep I'm worrying about, it's the cattle. I don't only run sheep. I've got heifers in that field over there' – he pointed – 'and cows down in that meadow.' He pointed again, then went on, 'And the second thing is, you don't light fires in the wood. You saw the wood we passed through down the road. Well, you can get as much dry tinder as you want down there, but you don't light fires there . . . understood?'

Slowly Matty nodded.

'And the third thing is, no yelling and carrying on after ten o'clock at night. Got that?'

Again Matty nodded, but slowly, rather bewilderedly. And then Mr Walsh finished by saying, 'Well, now you can enjoy yourselves.'

At this, Willie let out a small hoot of a laugh, and Matty was inclined to join him, but the expression on Mr Walsh's face warned him he had better not.

'Now, if I were you,' said Mr Walsh, pointing

63

to the kitbags, 'I'd get your tents up and your stuff put nice and tidy; then you can bring your can over to the house for your milk, and Mrs Walsh might find you a cup of tea.'

For the first time in their short acquaintance, Mr Walsh smiled. He smiled first at Willie, then at Joe, then at Matty. And as he went to walk away, he put out his hand and rumpled Joe's head.

'Coo! I thought for a minute he was old Bore all over again,' said Willie, 'until he said that bit about going across and his wife making us tea. Come on, fellows, hurry up.'

The tea, looking like a mirage before them, urged them to erect the tents and get their kit straight in an unbelievably short time, and when they were ready to go to the farm it was Matty, looking about him, who said, 'A can. We've forgotten to bring a can for the milk.'

'I've got that empty pop bottle,' said Willie.

'Well, that'll have to do,' said Matty.

Together, they went towards the farm, and as they passed through the gate Joe made a great ceremony of closing it, saying aloud, 'First rule, close the gate, me little man.'

'Ssh! Ssh!' said Matty. 'Don't take the micky; he may hear you.'

They were quiet as they approached the farm. Slowly, somewhat tentatively, they made their way to the back door. Matty knocked, and his knock was answered by a girl of about twelve years old. She had a round face, round, merry grey-green eyes, and long brown hair in a pony tail.

Looking over her shoulder, she cried, 'Mother, they're here.'

A woman now came towards the door. She was

small and plump and kindly-looking, and her voice furthered this impression, for, unlike her husband's, it was soft and slow. 'Come in,' she said. 'Come away in, boys. You've had a long journey.'

As they walked into the kitchen, it was Joe who found his tongue first. 'Yes, missus.' He nodded at her. 'We've come all the way from Tyne Dock.'

'Oh, that's a long way.'

As Matty watched her shake her head down at Joe he didn't know whether she was sympathizing with him, or laughing at him.

'What's your name?' she asked him.

'Joe, missus,' he said. 'Joe Darling.' His eyes flicked towards the girl as he spoke. Then addressing Mrs Walsh again, he laughed as he went on, 'It's a funny name. I get chipped about it.'

'I think it's a nice name, a name to be proud of. Don't forget Grace Darling.' She nodded at him again before she turned to Willie. 'And what's your name?'

'Willie Styles.' Willie gave her the whole treatment of his engaging grin.

'Willie Styles?' she repeated. 'Well, Willie, I hope you enjoy your holiday.'

'Thanks, missus.' He nodded his head at her.

'And you?' She was looking at Matty.

'I'm Matty Doolin.'

'Doolin? Oh, you're Irish?'

'Not really. Me granda was, that's all.'

'Well, I hope you have a nice holiday.' Mrs Walsh looked for some time at Matty, before she turned to her daughter and said, 'This is Jessica.' Then letting her glance travel over them all, she pulled a prim face as she added, 'And she doesn't like to be called Jessie.'

'Oh, mother!' As her daughter made this protesting statement Mrs Walsh said, 'Now, I'm sure you're all ready for a cup of tea. Well, it's mashed. Sit yourselves down. Are you hungry?'

'I'm always hungry, Mrs Walsh.' This was from Willie.

'Me, too,' put in Joe.

'And what about you?' Mrs Walsh turned her head towards Matty as she lifted the big, brown teapot from the hob of the open range. And Matty smiled at her before he said, 'Me mother says she used to know a corporation horse who used to eat like me.'

Matty felt pleased as he listened to Mrs Walsh laughing. It was a jolly laugh; it was as if she enjoyed laughing. He felt he had accomplished something. He watched her now go towards the long dresser against the far wall of the kitchen, and, lifting a cloth, disclose a number of plates laden with food. He watched her and Jessica bring them to the table, and he couldn't believe that she had prepared all this stuff for them.

'Sit up,' she said. 'Sit up.'

'Eeh! missus.' Joe was gazing at the laden plates of bread and butter, scones, tarts, and a huge bacon and egg pie adorning the centre of the table. As she put a cup of tea to the side of his plate he looked up at her and said brightly, 'Eeh! it's like being at Matty's mam's. Matty's mam's a good cook an' all.'

'Is she?' Mrs Walsh was looking towards Matty, and Matty proffered, 'She likes cooking.'

'So do I,' said Mrs Walsh. 'I also like to see what I've cooked eaten, so now tuck in, all of you.'

Mrs Walsh hadn't to repeat this order, and she hovered around them as they made good inroads on everything on the table.

66

Jessica sat at the far end of the table and watched them. This tended to make Matty feel embarrassed. He wished, at this moment, that Mrs Walsh had had a son instead of a daughter. But his thoughts were soon diverted from Jessica on seeing that Willie was bent on clearing every plate on the table. So he brought the meal to an abrupt end by rising to his feet and saying, 'Thank you, Mrs Walsh; that was a grand tea,' at the same time making an almost imperceivable movement with his hand towards the other two. Joe answered the signal at once, but Willie was hesitant, and when he finally rose to his feet his eyes lingered on all the food still left.

'You will want some milk,' said Mrs Walsh. 'Have you a can?'

'No,' piped up Joe; 'we forgot it, but we've got a bottle.'

Mrs Walsh looked towards the bottle, where Willie had left it on a table just inside the door, and she said, 'Oh! You don't want to put your milk in that, I'll lend you a can. How are you off for bread and stuff?'

'Oh, we've got piles of grub,' put in Joe. 'Matty's mother baked all yesterday and . . .'

'We'll only have enough bread to last us a couple of days, Mrs Walsh,' interrupted Matty; 'but we can go into the town . . . or the nearest place . . . and get some.'

'Well, the nearest place is Allendale.' Mrs Walsh was filling a quart can with milk from a larger one as she spoke. 'And that's nine miles away.'

'Coo! nine miles. That's some distance. We'll never be able to walk that.'

'There won't be any need,' said Mrs Walsh, putting the can on the table. 'My husband goes in to Hexham once a week, sometimes twice; you can go in with him.'

None of the boys showed any enthusiasm at the offer, and it was at this point that Jessica burst out laughing, and they all turned towards her. Her head was resting on her forearm on the table. Then she looked up at her mother as she said, 'Father must have been doing his gallop.'

'Oh!' Mrs Walsh shook her head. 'Did he drive very fast?'

'I'll say,' said Willie, grinning now. 'I'd have been over the side, b . . . but me eyebrows caught on the back.' Jessica laughed and Mrs Walsh, shooing them towards the door and speaking as if she had known them for years, said, 'Go on with you.' Then: 'And don't worry about the bread; I bake once a week and I'll put in a little extra for you.'

'Thanks, Mrs Walsh,' said Matty.

As they stepped into the yard Jessica went with them. 'You'll want a spade for digging your fireplace,' she said to Willie. 'I'll fetch one.'

'What's she mean? Dig a fireplace,' Joe whispered to Matty.

'You dig a hole to lay the fire in, chump,' said Matty.

'We never did,' said Willie, none too quietly. 'We made a square with bricks and put the fire in that.'

'Well, shut up! Here she comes,' hissed Joe.

'There.' Jessica handed the spade to Willie, but continued to walk with them.

Except for the comment of 'Coo! can't you see for miles,' from Joe, no one spoke until they reached the gate. And as Matty went to open it his attention was drawn to Willie. Willie was handing the spade to Joe, and to Matty's amazement he watched his tall lanky friend take a grip on the wall to the side of the gate and with a crouch and a spring lift himself over it. It was the same technique that he used on the horse in the gym. He was always very good at vaulting, and he had always given him credit for it, but not now. The big stiff was showing off because of a girl.

When Jessica and Joe had passed into the field, Matty banged the gate shut. They said that girls always jammed up the works, and he had a premonition that he was going to experience some jamming in the near future.

'Oh, you've got a lot of stuff.' Jessica was moving amongst the baggage. 'But only two tents?'

'Me and Matty sleep in the big one,' Joe pointed to it. Then turning to Matty, he exclaimed, 'We forgot to ask about the water . . . Where do we get water?' He looked at Jessica.

'From the stream.'

'Can't see no stream,' said Joe.

'It's round the hill. Come on, I'll show you.' As she turned from them and ran across the field, she was immediately followed by Willie and Joe. Matty's legs, too, made a number of strides before they stopped. Then slowly he turned back to the encampment. There was the fireplace to dig out; and anyway, he wasn't going to run all over the place after a girl.

It was almost ten minutes before they returned, and the boys came up panting and shouting. Then they all stood for a moment looking at the hole Matty had dug, until Jessica exclaimed, 'That's too big and too deep. And where have you put the turves?'

'The turves?' Matty looked down at her. 'The grass is under there.' He pointed to a pile of soil.

Jessica shook her head, a small superior smile on her face. 'You should always cut the turves off nice and neat and put them to one side, and, when you're leaving, fill in the hole and put the turves back. That's what the scouts do. There were some here last year and you couldn't tell where their fireplace had been when they left.'

Matty only just held back a retort that would have put both her and the scouts in their proper places, but, looking at the hole, he realized she was right . . . it was too big and too deep.

'You should start again, that'll never be right. I'd fill it in if I were you.'

'Aye, I think that's a good idea. I'd fill it in, Matty.' Willie nodded his head knowingly, and regretted it the next minute as the spade was thrust into his hand, and Matty said, 'Right, get it filled in. And then dig a fireplace and . . . put the turves to one side. I'm going to unpack the rest of the gear.'

Matty stalked away, and there was a telling silence all about the little camp until, on hands and knees, unpacking the Primus, which his father had said should only be used for early morning tea and on special occasions, he heard the hushed voice of Jessica asking, 'Is he always grumpy like that?' And his reactions were very mixed when he heard Joe's reply, 'Aye, but he's all right. Matty's all right.' Then Joe, apparently seeking agreement, said softly, 'Isn't he, Willie?' And it was no comfort to Matty to hear Willie's reply, 'Oh aye, Matty's all right. He's just made like that.'

Just made like that! Matty was bristling with indignation now. They were talking about him as if he was an oddity. Just because he didn't keep yapping all the time.

As Willie dug the hole under Jessica's direction, the three of them giggling together, Matty's feeling of isolation grew.

When, a while later, the dry sticks ignited and the flames shot upwards there was a cheer from Willie and Joe, and they cried to him, 'Look at this, Matty, a fire!'

Matty strode towards them, saying as nonchalantly as he could, 'Well, you've seen a fire afore, haven't you?'

'Aye.' Joe nodded at him. 'But not made like this. She's good, isn't she?' He jerked his head towards Jessica, who was disappointed when all the big stubborn-looking boy said was, 'A fire's not good unless there's something to put on it.'

'Did you bring any water with you from the stream?' Matty went on.

'No,' Willie shook his head. 'Forgot to take the bucket.'

'You would.' Matty turned away and, grabbing up the canvas bucket, went down the field in the direction that the boys had taken earlier. He had just rounded the foot of the hill when he heard flying footsteps, and Jessica caught him up.

'Look, I'll show you,' she said and ran past him down the gentle slope that led to the stream.

When Matty reached the bank, he stood looking down at the water running over the rocks, so crystal clear it was as if he were looking into a mirror. On the bank opposite grew the big leaves of the saxifrage, parsley fern, and foxgloves. These flourished thickly right up to a wall of rock. Slowly Matty raised his eyes to this, and saw tumbling down it the water that fed the stream. It was jingling, and tinkling, and gurgling like a happy child at play. He wished he was alone and could stand and look about him, and listen to the sound of the waterfall, for never in his life before had he seen such a beautiful sight as this stream that was fed from the rocks.

'You can wash here.' Jessica was pointing down to the water at their feet. 'But you get your drinking water from there.' She raised her hand upwards toward the rock. 'Look, I'll show you how to get it.' She was away from him and climbing the bank that was part of the rock face, and when she reached the top she leant against the moss-covered sloping wall and pushing the fingers of her right hand into a niche she stretched out her left hand towards the falling water, and it cascaded from it in a sparkling shower. Then, turning to him, she shouted, 'See!'

He nodded slowly, and when she came down to his side again she said, 'It's lovely water. I mean, to drink.'

He was looking about him, and more to himself than to her he said, 'It's lovely altogether, beautiful. I've never seen anything like it.'

'Really!' Her tone was full of quiet surprise.

He nodded. 'No, never. It's like a dream.' He lifted his head; first to the rock face and the tumbling water; then to the far flower-filled bank; and then beyond, to another valley sloping gently away and guarded in the far distance by yet more hills rising to mountains.

'It's nice in the summer, but in the winter – ugh!' Jessica shuddered. 'You're frozen, frozen.' She shook her hand. 'Your fingers drop off.'

He looked down at her now, and for the first time he smiled at her and said jocularly, 'Well, yours have grown again.'

She laughed. 'Oh, but you know what I mean.'

'Yes, I know what you mean.'

'Will I get the water for you?' Her voice was still quiet, and he answered, 'No, I'll get it meself.'

'It isn't easy.'

'Well, I'll have to find that out, won't I?' He softened this tart rejoinder with another smile. And then he climbed the rock, and, doing as she had done, he pressed himself against the face, found a hold for his right hand and held out the bucket with his left. As the water pinged into it he almost overbalanced and went over the edge. And Jessica's voice came to him, laughing now, 'I told you. I told you.'

When he pulled the bucket to him it was only quarter full. The water looked so gentle as it tumbled down, there didn't seem any force behind it, but when it hit anything it acted like a fast-running tap on a flat board and sprayed upwards.

'I told you. It's better with a jug, and then you can fill the bucket.'

He turned to her. 'I'll learn.' Again he pressed himself against the wall. Again he held out the bucket. Again he made a waterspout. And there was even less in the bucket when he drew it to him for the second time.

'You stay there and I'll dash up to the house and get a jug. I won't be long.' Before she had finished speaking she was away, running swiftly.

Slowly he lowered himself from the rock, and, going to the stream, sat on the bank, and stared at the racing water a few inches below his dangling feet. And as he stared there came upon him an intense longing to be alone in this place, really alone. The longer this feeling stayed with him the more guilty he felt, for it was making him wish that Joe and Willie were miles away, in fact back home in Tyne Dock.

73

As his eyes followed the stream to where it disappeared round a curve in the land, he said slowly to himself, 'I'll die in the docks.'

The next instant he was on his feet. He was daft. That's what he was, daft. He hadn't been here five minutes and he was making himself as miserable as if he were back at school. And why should he stay here anyway and wait for a girl to bring him a jug? He should have gone and got it himself. He strode away round the foot of the hill into the field . . . Anyway, taking orders from a girl . . . he wasn't going to start doing that.

4

They had a supper of sausages, fried potatoes, eggs, fried bread and cocoa, and all three laughed and joked as they ate. When the meal was finished, they lay on the grass, comfortably full, while they waited for the kettle to boil to do the washing up. They were lying facing the long valley. The sun had just dropped beyond a distant high peak and from its dying there gushed up a spray of orange, pink and mauve colour which spread across the sky like a soft tide, the edge of which was advancing towards them.

'It's bonny,' said Joe.

'Aye,' said Matty.

There was a pause. Then Willie asked, 'What'll we do the morrow, eh?' When he received no answer he repeated, 'I said, what will we do the morrow, Matty?'

'Oh, go for a hike.'

'Where?'

'Oh, I don't know. We should have got a map.'

'Mr Walsh will tell us where to go,' said Joe.

'Do you think she'll want to come along?'

Matty had raised himself sharply on his elbow, and, addressing Willie pointedly, he said, 'Well if she does or not she's not coming.'

'Well, I only thought . . .'

'She's only a kid, just on twelve.'

'O.K. O.K., Matty man, I know that. I was just sayin' . . .' There was an edge to Willie's voice now.

'Well, don't,' said Matty. 'She's not coming hikes with us. How far do you think she could walk?'

'Likely a sight farther than us.'

This telling statement from Joe brought Matty's eyes round to him, and caused him to smile as he said now, 'You're likely right there, but still' – his face became straight again – 'she's not comin'.'

'Dishes,' said Matty, as the long twilight began to deepen. Both Joe and Willie repeated the word, but prefixed with an 'Aw!' And Matty, too, getting reluctantly to his feet, said, 'Well, they've got to be done. And if we leave them till the morning the fat'll be as hard as nails . . .'

The dishes washed, and stacked under the spare ground sheet that was covering the oddments of their camp equipment, they all showed a great urgency to go to bed. Now followed an hilarious half-an-hour, during which Willie had them doubled up with laughter by wriggling his way out of his tent inside his sleeping bag, looking for all the world like a gigantic caterpillar.

But once in his sleeping bag, Joe found that whatever way he turned he was lying on a lump. This resulted in him getting out, lifting the ground sheet and battering his portion of earth with a stone which took him all his time to lift.

Matty's own strip of ground was flat, but hard. He didn't think he had felt anything so hard in his life, and he hoped his dad was right about the ground feeling as soft as a feather bed in the morning.

At last they were settled. Matty lay staring

out between the open flaps into the now dark night. There was not a sound to be heard. He thought if he listened hard he'd be able to hear the waterfall, but he couldn't. All his life he had gone to bed against the wall of background noises, for at night the docks had never really slept, the traffic had never ceased; and all around them, behind thin brick walls, were people. But here there was nothing; no sound whatever. He resisted the urge to speak to Joe, and the silence swelled and swirled in his head, and the thread of fear in him turned into a rope.

So when the figure, darker than the night, loomed in the doorway and spoke his name softly, saying, 'Matty,' it acted like an explosion under him, and he sat bolt upright, gasping.

'You weren't asleep, were you?' Willie's voice was hushed. 'Man, I can't get off, it's so quiet. Do you feel it quiet?'

Matty had to swallow a number of times before he could answer. And then he made his voice harsh as he said, 'Of course it's quiet; you're in the country.'

'It doesn't scare you?'

'No, of course it doesn't. You've been out campin' afore, haven't you?'

'Aye, I know, but never in the wilds like this. On the camp sites and such . . . Is he asleep?'

Before Matty could answer, Joe's thin voice piped up, 'No, I'm not. I felt it an' all. I listened for the cows mooing, or some noise from the farm, but it must be too far away . . . you not scared, Matty?'

'Scared!' Matty's voice was high. 'Don't be daft. Go on and lie down. And you, Willie, get back into your bag. I'm dog tired and want to get asleep.'

77

'O.K.' Willie sounded lost as he turned away, and Joe said, 'It's sleeping on his own. I'm glad I'm not.'

'Go to sleep,' said Matty. 'Good-night.'

'Good-night, Matty.'

Matty lay down, feeling really very tired now. The fear had gone; he no longer heard the silence. The others felt like he did. He felt as warm as toast; that was the double eiderdown inside the sleeping bag. He thought vaguely of his mother as sleep came to him. She'd be worrying. Aye, she'd be worrying the night.

When morning came, the silence of the night was forgotten for the air was filled with the deep mooing of the cattle, the sharp intermittent barking of a dog in the distance, and the unusual sound of a breeze stirring the top of the long grass.

They cooked bacon, fried bread, and sausages for their breakfast, and when they found the sausages were slightly more than high they laughed as they peppered the stone wall with them.

It was around half-past ten when, washed and tidy, they made their way to the farm, there to be greeted by Mr Walsh. He was standing at the door of the cow byres, and called to them, 'Well, your first night over. How did it go?'

'Oh, fine, fine.' They went towards him, and as they came up he asked, 'Not disturbed or anything?'

'Disturbed?' Joe shook his head. 'It was too bloomin' quiet.'

'Quiet?' Mr Walsh pulled a long face. 'Well, I suppose it's all a matter of comparison. It's quiet to where you came from. Well now, you after some milk?' He addressed Matty who was carrying the can, but Matty was looking past him into the cow byre and needed a push from Joe to recall his attention to what Mr Walsh was saying. And then he exclaimed, 'Oh, milk! Yes, please. We were just going to ask Mrs Walsh about it.'

'Oh. She and Jessica have gone up to church, but give me your can here and I'll fill it from the churn.' As he took the can from Matty's hand he paused a moment before saying, 'Would you like to look round?'

'Oh. Yes, please.'

'Aye. Yes.' It was a chorus from the other two.

'Well then, come along.' He went before them into the cow shed, pushing at the rump of a cow as he passed her, saying, 'Move over, Dolly.'

'Ooh, look!' Joe had stopped and was pointing to a cow. 'It's being milked by one of them machines.'

'Yes,' said Mr Walsh. 'Machines help a lot these days when you can't get labour.'

'How many cows have you?' asked Matty.

'Seven,' said Mr Walsh. 'Seven milkers. And then I've got ten heifers, and a bull.'

'A bull!' put in Willie. 'Is he loose?'

'No, lad.' Mr Walsh slanted his eyes up towards Willie. 'But if you want to go in for training I'll let him out.'

Willie saw the joke as did the others. Then Mr Walsh said, 'I'll be with you in a minute; I must take her off.' Returning to the cow that was being milked, he took away the apparatus. Then with the pail of frothing milk in his hand, he went into the dairy. They followed him and stood gaping at the stark whiteness and cleanliness around them.

Matty, wide-eyed, watched Mr Walsh measure the milk, then jot down an entry in a book lying on a marble slab.

'There, that's that.' Mr Walsh turned to the boys. 'That's my milking over for a few hours. Just a minute.' He went back into the cow shed, and, lifting up a hose from a hook, he turned on a tap and swilled a line of cow dung into a trough that ran along the length of the byres. In a minute or so he was back, saying, 'Well now, come and see the rest of the animals.'

In the farmyard once more, Mr Walsh pointed to a large shed-like structure with an open front, open, that is, except for a low fence. Beyond the fence were two sheep.

'I'm keeping them quiet for a day or two,' explained Mr Walsh. 'One got its hoof ripped on a broken bottle.' He turned and pointed to Joe. 'That's what comes of throwing bottles and stuff away after picnics.'

Joe grinned up at him. 'It wasn't me.'

'No.' There was a similar grin on Mr Walsh's face now. 'But it might have been, eh?'

'What do you use this for?' asked Matty, pointing into the enclosure.

'For the sheep in the winter, in rough weather like it was a year or so back. Remember? Times like that we bring as many in as we can. When they are lambing, that is. And this . . .' He moved on as he spoke and went towards the door, the upper half of which was open and showed a large room walled by bins. 'This is where we keep the grain and feed.'

'Smells nice.' Joe sniffed as he strained his head over the bottom part of the door.

They came next to a big barn, the doors open wide. As Matty stood behind the others looking into the barn, he thought that, were his mother here she would say, 'That's a conglomeration of stuff and no mistake,' for the barn appeared to be

80

full of nothing but parts of old machinery: an old tractor, red with rust, what looked like the inside of a motor, and wheels, large and small wheels. If it hadn't been for the bales of hay in the far corner the place could have been taken for a garage workshop.

Mr Walsh dismissed the conglomeration with a wave of his hand, saying, 'I'll have to get down to that some day, but the time flies, never seem to get a minute. It's always the same on a farm.'

Now he was leading his way along an alley between the side of the barn and the stone building and into another yard that opened on to a field. One side of this yard was taken up with pig sties, and the boys all laughed as they looked into the first sty and saw ten piglets scrambling over the sow before arranging themselves in an orderly row to feed.

'Coo!' said Willie, his face one big grin. 'That's what's meant by sucking pig.'

They moved on to stand looking over a gate into a field full of chickens.

'That's a swarm,' said Joe, 'there must be over a hundred there.'

'Make it two and you'll be nearer the mark,' said Mr Walsh.

Mr Walsh next led the way down by the stone wall to another gate, and, leaning on it, he pointed to the animal grazing quietly in the middle of the field as he said, 'There's the boss.'

'Eeh! isn't he big?' said Willie.

'Is that the bull?' said Joe.

'That's the bull,' said Mr Walsh. 'And he's called Sep.'

'Why do you call him that?' Joe was laughing up into Mr Walsh's face, and Mr Walsh, still looking at the bull, said, 'Well, I called him that because he's got the same temperament as me father, and his name was Septimus. If you overstepped the mark or took any liberties with me father you found yourself in a horizontal position. It's the same with him.' He pointed. 'He knows his place, and if you give it to him, well and good; take any liberties, and you're on your back.' Mr Walsh looked from one to the other, and after a pause added, 'And that's a warning. Never try any tricks with Sep. If you should be round this way and he happens to be near the gate, your wisest plan is to raise your cap to him and walk sedately on.'

This last brought a high laugh from Willie and Joe and a smile from Matty. Matty was studying Mr Walsh. He thought he was a funny man, not funny peculiar, or funny ha-ha, as the saying went, just funny; and it came to him that you'd have to be careful how you trod when walking near Mr Walsh, so-to-speak. He also came to the conclusion that Mr Walsh was like his dad, and they were both, in some way, akin to the bull.

'You haven't got much to say for yourself?'

The abrupt statement shot at Matty startled him, and he said quickly, 'I . . . I was looking round; there's so much to see.'

'He's nearly always quiet, Mr Walsh. Just now and again, he lets go,' said Joe.

The fact that he was under discussion made Matty hot and uncomfortable, and he turned his head away and looked along the road by the stone wall. And what he saw at the far end brought his body round immediately and he cried spontaneously, 'Why, look!' He pointed to where two sheep dogs were ambling leisurely towards them. 'You've got dogs?' said Matty, looking at Mr Walsh.

'We've got dogs?' repeated Mr Walsh. 'Of course we've got dogs. A sheep farm would be very badly off without dogs. You'd need ten pairs of legs if you hadn't dogs. What makes you surprised at that?'

'Oh, nothing. Nothing. I . . . well.' He floundered and turned his gaze to the dogs again.

The two sheep dogs came up, wagging their tails, and Willie and Joe immediately went down on their hunkers, crying, 'Here! Boy. Here! Boy,' as their hands ruffled the dogs' fur.

Matty did not drop to his hunkers but stood looking down on the animals, while Mr Walsh looked at him.

It was the bigger of the two dogs that disengaged itself rather peremptorily from Willie's fussing hands and came to sniff at Matty's legs. And when the dog looked up at him, Matty bent down and, rubbing his hand slowly and lovingly behind the dog's ear, said, 'Hello there, boy.'

'It's a bitch, and her name's Betsy.'

Matty didn't remark on Mr Walsh's information but continued to rub the dog's ear gently. And after a moment, he said, 'Good Betsy. Good Betsy.'

'What's this one called?' Joe was fondling the smaller of the two dogs.

'He's called Prince. He's Betsy's son, and she's in the course of training him. He's just on two years old.'

'How old is Betsy?' Matty was still looking at the dog.

'Oh, she's getting on. She's around seven. And that's funny.' Mr Walsh was peering at Matty. 'She doesn't usually let people fuss her like that; she's an independent creature as a rule.'

'I like dogs.' Matty's voice was soft, and his eyes didn't leave the dog's face as he spoke.

'He's barmy about dogs, Mr Walsh.' Joe was nodding down at Matty. 'That's why we're here. His mother wouldn't have let him come campin', but it was through her his dog was killed . . . run over, and she . . .'

'It wasn't.' Matty was on his feet, his voice a growl now. 'It wasn't her fault. And shut your mouth, it's all finished.'

'Here! Here! Young fellow, me lad. There's no need to go off the deep end like that.' Mr Walsh's voice was harsh. 'The young 'un was only explaining something to me. You want to control that temper, boy, or it'll cause you trouble one of these days . . . Well now, I've got to get on with me work. Come along with you all.'

They followed him quietly. The harmony of the morning was shattered, but when they reached the main farmyard again Mr Walsh asked them, in an ordinary tone, 'What are you going to do with yourselves the day?'

'We thought of going for a hike,' said Willie. 'We were goin' to ask you which was the best place to go.'

'Oh, well.' Mr Walsh ran his hand through his hair. 'You want to take things quietly at first. Have you done any climbing?'

'No.' Willie and Joe shook their heads.

'Well then, don't bite off more than you can chew the first day. If I were you I wouldn't try to climb any hills or mountains. I would go to the end of this road, you know where we turned off the other day, cross over it and you'll come to a path that leads you under the railway bridge. That's about another mile or so on. From anywhere round there you'll get a good view of

Tindale Tarn and Cold Fell. But I'd make that view all you take in today. You'll have plenty of time within the next fortnight to climb, and there's more than enough climbing material round about. There's Blacklow Hill, Carrick, and Black Fell, all over yon side of the river.'

'What river is it, Mister?' asked Joe.

'Well, for a good part of the way it's the South Tyne, until it peters out. That's on that side. Then, on this side, there's the West Allen river and' – he waved his hand in the air now – 'and that's enough to get on with the day. Get yourselves away now and have a good time. And don't forget your milk.'

It was Matty who picked up the milk can, and it was he who left the yard first, the other two walking some way behind him. But as they entered the field Joe came up and said under his breath, 'I'm sorry, Matty. I meant nowt; no harm or owt.' There was a long pause before Matty answered, 'I know that. Only ... only I don't want me mam blamed. It was my fault; I should have taken him as she told me, and then he wouldn't have been hurt.'

'Oh, it wasn't your fault, man,' Willie put in. 'You only did what you thought best for the dog. But anyway, let's forget it. Come on, let's put some chuck together and get going.' He punched at Matty. Then Joe punched at him, and Matty, his face breaking into a grin, cried, 'Give over the pair of you; you'll have the milk spilt.'

So they set out on their first hike, whistling, chatting, and laughing as they went along.

5

It was around four o'clock in the afternoon that
the trio, no longer whistling or laughing, stopped
for a rest on the perilous part of the road where it
dropped sheer into the valley. They were once
again tired, hot, thirsty and hungry, and to add
to these inflictions Willie had become a casualty.
For the first time in his life he was experiencing
a blistered heel. The fact that the blister had
broken added to his discomfort, which he made
verbal at every limping step.

'Look, tie another hankie around it,' suggested
Matty. 'And put your shoe on again; you'll get
along better.'

'I can't, man, it's agony. You don't know, your
feet's all right, so you can talk.'

'You'll have to soak it in the stream when we
get back,' said Matty.

'Aw, yes, when we get back. When will that be?
If you hadn't wanted to see round the next hill,
and the next, we'd never have gone so far.'

'All right! All right!' Matty was snapping back
now, and at this moment Joe cried, 'Look what's
comin'. Look, there.' He was pointing excitedly
down the twisting road. 'It's Mr Walsh's lorry.'

'Aye, it is. You're saved.' Matty could now
smile down at Willie, where he was sitting on the
grass verge.

In a few minutes the lorry came up to them, and Mr Walsh, leaning over the wheel, surveyed them with a twinkle of humour in his eye before saying, 'You're all dead beat, you've got sore feet, and you'll never do it again.'

'Aye, that's about it, Mr Walsh.' Matty smiled self-consciously up at him. 'Though Willie's come off worst; he's got a skinned heel.'

'Oh.' Mr Walsh let himself slowly down from the cab and went to where Willie was supporting himself on one foot. 'Well. Well. Well.' He appraised the bare heel. 'It looks a sore one that.'

The sympathy brought Willie stammering and spluttering. 'Aye. It . . . it . . . it is. It's awful, Mr Walsh. I've never had anything wr . . . wrong with me feet afore . . .'

'Well, you've been lucky, lad. If you're going walking the fells this won't be the last blister you'll have, not by a long chalk, and certainly not if you wear shoes like that.' He pointed disdainfully to the pointed-toed shoe Willie held in his hand. 'What possessed you to go walking in shoes like that? You want boots for fell walking; something to support the ankle, and a good stout sole.' He looked from Joe's feet to Matty's and remarked, 'Now those are sensible. Although they could do with a much stouter sole. As for yours, me little fellow,' – he jerked his head at Joe – 'they're not much better than your pal's.'

As he helped Willie up into the back of the lorry, Mr Walsh said, 'It was lucky for you I decided to drop over to Slaggyford. I've a brother-in-law over there who's not too well. It's an ill wind.'

'Aye, it is.' Joe nodded knowingly at Mr Walsh.

It was apparent to Matty that Mr Walsh liked

Joe. He also thought he had a sneaking regard for
Willie. Most people liked Willie because he could
make them laugh. But he had an idea that Mr
Walsh hadn't cottoned on to himself.

When the lorry stopped opposite the field gate,
Mr Walsh pulled open the sliding window in the
back of the cab, and, looking at Willie, said, 'You
stay put and let Mrs Walsh dress that heel for
you. You others nip over the side; I'm not coming
round.'

The next minute Matty and Joe were standing
on the roadway watching the lorry carrying their
now smug-faced pal towards the farm.

'I bet she gives him tea.' This was from Joe.

'Aye, I bet she does,' said Matty. 'And he'll
play his sore heel as if it was his guitar – not that
he's any hand at that.'

They laughed weakly as they went into the
field and Joe said, 'Talkin' about guitars, when
his mother wouldn't let him bring it he was a bit
wild, but he brought his mouth organ.'

'He did!' Matty stopped. 'Well, he'd better not
play it after ten o'clock, that's all. Come on.'

With a spurt of energy they ran towards the
camp which had suddenly taken on the appearance of home to them both.

Matty lay in his sleeping bag, his hands behind
his head, staring at the roof of the tent. To his
side, Joe, resting on his elbow, peered towards
him. They were both listening to Willie's voice
coming from his tent, for at least the tenth time,
explaining to them about his late return.

'It wasn't my fault, man, I tell you; I couldn't
refuse the tea, could I? And then, when they had
company and they got talkin' and . . .'

There now came the concerted chorus from

Matty's tent, as both he and Joe cried, 'And I made them laugh.' This was followed by a derisive: 'Tell us the old, old story.' Then Matty added, 'All right. You've told us a dozen times, so let it drop. What's wrong with you is not only a sore heel but a sore conscience. As I said afore, you were stuffin' your kite with fancies knowing we just had bread and jam and the end of me mam's cake.'

Silence followed this remark, and the two boys, looking at each other in the reflected light from the bright moonlight outside, nodded their heads once, then burrowing down in their bags, they lay quiet.

It must have been ten minutes later when Matty, almost on the point of sleep, heard Willie's voice as if he were talking to himself, saying in self-pitying tones, 'I get the backwash of everythin'. It's Willie this, an' Willie that. I'll likely get the blame for the hole the morrow.'

On this last remark Matty pressed his lips tightly together to prevent himself from making a retort, for the matter of the hole still rankled.

It hadn't been Willie's staying at the farm until nine o'clock that had got his back up so much as their finding the hole, the new hole, on their return, and the sausages lying in a heap near the ashes of the fire. The hole was just over a spade's width each side and about a foot deep, and it was a beautifully cut hole. As he had stood looking down on to what he later learned was called a grease pit, the top neatly criss-crossed with twigs and covered lightly with bracken, he had felt the hole to be a personal affront. SHE was showing him up.

The feeling did not lessen with the knowledge that she was right . . . And then those sausages.

89

He should never have left them lying about; he should have put them on the fire in the first place. Still he wasn't going to take it from her. She was only a kid, and too bossy by half. She should mind her own business, and he would tell her so. Aye, he would, when he saw her.

All evening he had waited for a visit from her, but when she didn't put in an appearance his feeling of annoyance grew. Joe had wanted them to go across to the farm, but he had been firm against that. They weren't going to do any sucking up; there were enough at that game already, he had said.

But Matty was tired now, and not a little footsore, so, soon, defecting pals, bossy girls, and the worries of life in general slid from him as he fell into a deep, untroubled sleep . . .

What the time was when the sound of a scream brought him sitting bolt upright, and Joe into spluttering, frightened awareness, he didn't know. Before the second yell ended they had both tumbled out of their bags, and as Matty, scrambling on hands and knees, emerged from the tent, Willie's voice came at him, stuttering, 'M . . . Matty! O . . . oh! M . . . Matty. Where are you, Matty?'

There was no moon now, only a cold dense blackness. If they'd had the wits to question they would have asked why it was so intensely cold after being such a fine day. Pulling his pyjama coat across his bare chest, Matty shouted, 'What's up, man? Where are you?' He made for the direction of Willie's tent, but Willie's voice came from somewhere near the wall, crying, 'I'm here!'

'Well, where's that? And what's the matter with you? Have you gone stark, staring bonkers?'

'It was a th ... th ... thing. It st ... started to wo ... worry me, man.'

'Get the torch, Joe.' Matty turned his head to where he thought Joe was, and Joe's voice came back at him, saying, 'Eeh! an' I'll get me coat an' all. I'm freezin'.'

A minute or so later, Joe crawled from the tent, flashing the light about him.

'Give it here,' said Matty.

'And here's your coat. Put it on,' said Joe.

Matty got gratefully into the coat. Then turning the flashlight towards the wall, he saw Willie; and, going quickly towards him, he said, 'Come on, get back into your tent. You'll be froze to death. What's up with you, anyway? You had a nightmare?'

'N ... no, man, no.' Willie's tone was emphatic now. 'I tell you, I was attacked by somethin'.'

'Oh, don't be daft.'

'I'm not daft. It tried to bite me lug off.'

If Willie could have seen Matty's expression and his rolling eyes he would have cried, 'You don't believe me?' As it was he said, 'It's a fact, man. I'm tellin' you. I woke up and there was this hairy thing, great big hairy thing, and it nearly took me ear.'

'Man, you've been dreamin'. Mean to tell me it came into the tent and bit your ear? Is your tent down?'

'No ... o! No.'

They were walking towards Willie's tent now. 'Yes see, it was kind of stuffy an' I lay with me head the other way ... outside.'

Matty was now flashing a light on the ground outside the tent, and, stooping down, he picked up about a third of a slice of bread with a piece of

91

meat adhering to it, and, keeping the torch flashed full on, he handed it to Willie.

'Well, man, it was only a sandwich. Mrs Walsh gave me one. If she had given me two I would have handed them over, but she only give me the one for me supper like.'

'And you were stuffin',' said Joe, 'an' you fell asleep. You know, you're a gutsy . . .'

'I'm not. I . . .'

'Here.' Matty thrust the dirty bread into Willie's hand. 'Take it and finish it, but do it inside 'cos the next animal that comes huntin' round might take a fancy to your nose. And good luck to it.'

'Aw, Matty, don't be like that.'

'What do you expect me to be like?'

'I'm sorry, man, I'm sorry about gettin' you both up, but I was scared to death. Eeh! it was awful, man.' There followed a silence now and Willie, evidently shivering with the cold, as his stammering indicated, said, 'C . . . can I c . . . come along of you's?'

'No, you bloomin' well can't,' said Matty emphatically. 'There's hardly room for the two of us.'

'B . . . but, man, I'll never get to sleep. It scared me. Honest. C . . . can I just sit up in the c . . . corner.'

'Oh, for crying out loud. Get your bed and go in with Joe, and I'll take your tent.'

'Th . . . th . . . thanks, Matty.' As Willie went hurriedly into his tent to gather up his bag, Joe, going with Matty towards their tent, said, 'What did you want to do that for?'

'You want to get to sleep tonight, don't you?' said Matty.

'I'm not so sure I can now. You know somethin'?' They were inside the tent now. 'I wish we were on our own, Matty; he's nowt but a nuisance. I never thought he'd be like this. Me dad always says the bigger they are the softer they are . . . Aw, I wasn't hitting at you, Matty. You know that.'

'Shut up and get into bed. And if he starts nattering, don't answer him. Mind, I'm telling you. He might be frightened now but tomorrow morning it'll all be one big laugh, you'll see.'

And in the morning Joe saw.

Willie was in high fettle, and both Matty and Joe, being ordinary boys, and filled now with a good breakfast of porridge, bacon and eggs, and the coldness of the night forgotten in the warmth of the sun, were laughing with and at Willie's description of the midnight attack. Willie was now lying on his side, curled up, giving a demonstration of being asleep, at the same time manipulating one hand into an imitation of the pawing animal approaching his face. Then, his hand making a grab at his ear, he sprang up, yelling and dancing like a hottentot. It was at this point of the performance that Mr Walsh put his head over the wall.

'Well now.' He nodded towards Willie. 'That's a sure sign your heel's better.'

'Oh, aye, Mr Walsh. Yes. Yes, it's a lot better. I was just showin' them how I was attacked in the night by something . . . an animal.'

They all went towards the wall and the farmer. 'You were?' Mr Walsh's brows came down over his merry eyes, which gave the lie to his straight countenance.

'Aye, Mr Walsh. I was lyin' there . . .' Again Willie went through the pantomime of the attack, but before he had quite finished Joe took it up, saying, 'And he was screamin' like a girl, Mr Walsh, and brought us out into the freezing cold. Coo! We were nearly starved. And then he wouldn't sleep by himself.' He poked at Willie. 'That's the big fellow for you, he was frightened.'

'Well, you were all right, you hadn't been attacked,' said Willie. 'I could have lost me ear.'

'Lost your ear?' Joe's voice was derisive. 'He was stuffing himself, Mr Walsh, and must have fallen asleep while he was doing it, an' some animal came round, just sniffin'. That's what happened.'

'Yes.' Mr Walsh was smiling broadly. 'That's exactly what must have happened. It was likely a fox. Yet I can't see him going near your face.'

'Oh,' put in Joe quickly, his grin wide, 'he's got the kind of face a fox would like, Mr Walsh.'

They were all laughing now, Willie included. Then Mr Walsh, pointing towards the hole, said, 'I saw you hadn't a grease pit, so I dug you one. That's for all your dirty water, tea leaves and the like. You renew the bracken each day. And you always burn the top and all old food.' He was looking straight at Matty as he spoke, and he went on, 'And I've pegged out a space in the wood over there. I think you need a latrine, don't you?'

'Yes, yes, Mr Walsh.' Matty's voice was quiet, and his manner respectful. Yet he was angry inside for he knew he was being rebuked, even if in a nice way, for not running his camp properly.

'And what are your plans for today?' the farmer asked kindly now.

'Well, we can't go for a hike,' said Joe, 'because of Willie's foot. We just thought about stickin' around. Didn't we, Matty?'

Matty nodded. 'Yes, there's plenty of places to see round about.'

'Can we come over to the farm and look round again, Mr Walsh?' piped up Joe.

'Well, yes. If you don't get in the way, that is.'

'Oh, we won't get in the way,' Joe assured him. 'And thanks, Mr Walsh.'

Mr Walsh now turned from the boys and whistled, and the next minute they saw the two sheep dogs come racing from a fell in the distance. And when they were bounding round their master's legs, Matty dared to ask, 'Could we take them for a walk some time, Mr Walsh?'

'What! Take these dogs for a walk.' Mr Walsh laughed. 'It'll be the other way I think; they'll take you. Why, would you like to go out with them?'

'Oh yes,' said Matty. Mr Walsh stared at him for a moment before saying, 'Well then, when you're all ready for a hike again you'll have to come over the fells with them and see them at work. I'll be moving some sheep down the valley towards the end of the week.'

'Thanks. Thanks.' Matty nodded his head. His eyes looked bright, his face alive. Mr Walsh kept his gaze fixed on him again for some time before turning away and remarking abruptly, 'Aye. Well, this won't do. And don't forget about that lat, mind.'

'No, Mr Walsh.' Both Willie and Joe chorused after him, although it was to Matty the order had been given.

'So she never did it.' Joe was speaking below his breath, looking up at Matty, and Willie asked, 'Did what?'

'We thought Jessica had dug the hole,' said Joe.

'Aw, no, her dad did it.'

'Well, we know now, 'cos we've just been told. But don't say that you didn't think she did it.'

'I never thought about it at all,' said Willie candidly. 'Nor digging a lat either. Can't see the point of that.'

Matty refrained from adding his comments to this. Willie was the one who was supposed to know all about camping. Willie had been camping on his own, and with others. He knew the rules from A to Z. That is, when he had been discussing them in the schoolyard or in their back-yard. Now Matty realized he knew less about real camping than he did himself.

Matty had been in the cubs. He had also been in the scouts for a short time. Not long enough to experience camping out, yet his own sense should have told him, he chided himself, that they needed a grease pit and a lat. It wouldn't have mattered if the grease pit hadn't been done so meticulously as the one Mr Walsh had cut as long as there had been a hole, into which to drain their slops.

Matty was in two minds about going round the farm again. Not that he didn't want to explore every nook and cranny of it, but somehow he didn't want to come up against Mr Walsh. Mr Walsh could laugh and make a joke, but there was a side to him that appeared all eyes, and that side, Matty felt, was looking at him all the while.

Later on, when they had cleared up and made themselves presentable, Matty said, 'You two go on over, I think I'll go down to the stream and have a plodge.'

'Aw no,' protested Joe straightaway, 'I'm not going without you.'

'Me neither,' put in Willie. 'We all go, or we all stay.'

96

In an odd way, Matty felt comforted by this declaration of camaraderie and he said hastily, 'All right, we won't argue. Come on, let's get going.'

There was no sign of Mrs Walsh on the farm, nor yet of Jessica, but they saw a good deal of Mr Walsh. They passed him several times in their aimless wanderings. The aimlessness was much more apparent in Willie and Joe than in Matty. Matty would have liked to stand longer staring at the cows, the pigs, the chickens, and, from a good distance, the bull, but Willie and Joe kept moving on. Round and round the yard they sauntered, through the alleyway to the yard where the pigs were, across the field to the chicken run, then back again to the big barn.

When for the third time they entered the dairy, Mr Walsh, coming behind them, said abruptly, 'You fellows want a job?'

'Oh, yes, yes.' The chorus was quick and general.

'Well now, it's nothing fancy, and you'll likely get yourselves mucked up, but there's no dirt on a farm that water won't wash off. So, over to the shed there.' He pointed across the yard. 'You'll find some long prong forks and you can amuse yourselves on the heap.'

Joe, about to dart across the yard, stopped and said,

'That big pile in the other yard? The manure heap? You mean the manure heap?'

'The very same.' Mr Walsh's face looked quite expressionless. 'It wants turning. It'll give off a bit of steam, but that won't hurt you.'

Mr Walsh now stood looking to where the three boys were going into the shed, and he smiled to himself. He'd had long experience in getting rid of unwanted company around his farm. There was no need to be uncivil, just put a fork in their hands and send them to the manure heap. He jerked his chin upwards and turned quickly into the dairy to hide the expanding grin on his face.

'Well, that's the last time you'll get me on that lark.' Joe was hanging over the bank of the stream sloshing his shorts in the running water. 'And this the only pair of shorts I've got. I'll have to wear me long pants now.'

'You can cut the bottoms off,' said Willie with a laugh. He, too, was lying on the bank. But it was his shirt he was washing, and he held it by the collar and let the rushing water fill it out.

Further along the bank Matty was rubbing away at his socks.

'Do you know something?' he said. 'Do you know why he set us on that heap?' He watched them as they shook their heads at him. 'He wanted to get rid of us.'

'Get rid of us!' Joe's face was screwed up.

'Aye, I saw him at least three times having a peep at us. I figure that he thought we wouldn't last out ten minutes, what with the smell, and the steam, and the weight of the stuff, and those forks nearly twice as big as you.' He pushed at Joe, and Joe fell on to his side, and from that position he said, 'No kiddin', Matty. You think that's why he did it?'

'Sure. We've got all our things mucked up, haven't we? We've got to wash them. And even me, I've got a blister on me hand. Look.' He held out his palm.

'But you kept on the longest,' said Willie.

'I only kept on,' said Matty, 'just to show him.

I thought to meself I'll let him see what the lads from the Tyne can do, and when Joe here kept digging away I could see he was puzzled. But mind' – Matty again pushed at Joe – 'he couldn't see the size of the lumps you had on that fork. Big as peas some of them.'

'Well, he won't put us on that again. We don't want to stop going over,' said Willie.

'No?' said Joe in a high squeaking voice. 'Well, if you want to visit, you visit. If you want to see Jessica, you go.'

'Aw, man, don't be daft. Who wants to see Jessica?'

'You do.' Joe poked his face at him. But now he was grinning. 'And I wouldn't mind seein' her either if her mam invited me to tea every time. Oh no, I wouldn't mind staying in the kitchen. But as for jaunts round the farm . . . no, thanks. What you say, Matty?'

Matty lying on his back now, his hands under his head, staring up to where white tufts of cloud seemed to be resting on the tops of distant peaks, said dreamily, 'I wouldn't mind turning manure, no; I enjoyed it. It's only a stink if you think so.'

Behind him, Joe and Willie sat back on their hunkers and looked at each other with widening eyes.

6

It became so hot as the afternoon wore on that the boys, donning their trunks, lay on the stones in the shallow stream and splashed and larked about. At one period they were making so much noise that they weren't aware they had a visitor, and Matty, raising himself from his place in the foot of water where he had been pretending to swim, looked towards the bank, to see Jessica standing there.

'Oh, hello.' He pulled himself on to his hands and knees, but didn't rise. Then, turning his head, he shouted, 'Give over, you two.'

Lower down the stream, Willie and Joe stopped their capers and came scrambling up towards Matty.

'You all look lovely and cool.' Jessica laughed down on them. 'Did you find it cold at first?'

'Freezin'.' Joe shivered. 'That's when we first got in, but it's lovely now.'

'There's a place where you can swim near the river.'

'No kiddin'.' Willie was leaning against the bank now, looking up at her. 'How far is it?' He sounded excited.

'Not very far, just over a mile-and-a-half.'

Joe closed his eyes. 'Just over a mile-and-a-half, she said.'

'Could we get there by road?' It was Matty asking the question, and Jessica looked at him as she answered, 'That would take you twice as long. It would be quicker if you followed the stream.'

'Do you swim there?' asked Willie.

Jessica shook her head. 'Not unless my father's with me. It's very deep, and there's rocks all round; you've got to be careful. They call it Satan's Hole.'

'What do they call it that for?' asked Joe.

'Oh. Because some people were drowned there. A boy and a girl, one holiday.'

'Well, that's nice to know,' said Willie brightly. 'Let's go straight down.'

They all laughed at this. And then Jessica said, 'You'd better not today. My father sent me down to tell you there's a storm coming up and you'd better see to your tents.'

'A storm?' Joe put his head back on his shoulders and looked up into the clear sky. 'Why, it doesn't look like a storm here.'

'It does over the hills, and it's black behind the house. And because of the heat these last few days it'll be a bad one.'

'That's something to look forward to.' Willie had pulled himself on to the bank and was pressing the water from his hair as he looked down on Jessica. But she paid no attention to him; she addressed herself pointedly to Matty as she went on, 'Father says you should get yourselves a meal prepared quickly, and take as much stuff inside your tents as you can. And put your clothes where they won't get wet.' As she waited for a response from Matty, she continued to stare down on him, and after a moment he jerked his head at her and said gruffly, 'Thank your da . . . your father. Tell him we'll do what he says.'

'All right. I've got to go now; I'm helping mother in the dairy.' She flashed a bright smile from one to the other; then, turning abruptly, she ran from them.

Matty, on the bank now, said to the others, 'Well, come on. Get into your clothes.'

'I don't see what all the rush is for. And you know something?' Joe waved his towel towards Matty. 'I think Mr Walsh thinks we're numbskulls; he's always telling us what to do.'

'Well, let's face it.' Matty was pulling on his shorts. 'We are numbskulls. At this game anyway. And as far as he's concerned we've never done anything to prove him wrong, have we?'

'Yes, but if we'd not camped near a farm we'd have found these things out for ourselves, wouldn't we?'

'Yes, that's right,' Willie endorsed.

'Oh, be quiet the pair of you and get into your things, and come on.'

Matty was halfway up the field towards their camp when the light around him changed. It was as if somebody had turned a lamp down, from a bright clear flame to a dull flicker. There was no horizon in front of him, and when he reached the encampment and looked in the direction of the farm, although he couldn't see it, he knew it was lying under a low black cloud, and this cloud was moving rapidly towards him. Everything about him was quiet, and although the sun was no longer visible it was much hotter than it had been before. Hurriedly, he began gathering up their blankets and sleeping bags, which they had laid out to air, and as Willie and Joe came up the hill he called to them, 'Put a move on, will you? Put a move on.'

'By! It's hot. Eeh! Man, I'm sweatin'.' Willie came panting up to Matty's side.

'I've rolled your kit up.' Matty pointed. 'Get it inside. And yours, an' all, Joe.'

'Mr Walsh said we should have a meal, didn't he?' said Willie, as he went into his tent.

And Joe called after him, 'You and your belly! It's too hot to eat.'

Matty, too, shouted to Willie, who was still in his tent, 'What you doing in there? Come on, get a brick and knock your pegs in, and loosen the guy ropes.'

Coming out of his tent, Willie said, 'We should have the tents together. It would be better.'

'We're not having the tents together. I told you this morning we weren't. You keep jabbering until dawn. If you want company you can go in with Joe again, and I'll take yours.'

Joe, a food tin under one arm and a loaf under the other, going towards his tent, spoke as if to himself saying, 'Joe's got no say in this. Joe's just the shuttlecock.'

'Poor old Joe!' shouted Matty after him. 'And don't take that loaf in there like that. Bring it back and cut some bread, and butter it. Then open that tin of corned beef.'

'But I don't feel hungry, Matty man; I don't feel I want to eat again.'

'That's what you feel like now, but if you've got to sit in there for hours' – he thumbed in the direction of the tent – 'it'll be a different tune. There's no room inside to start cutting bread and preparing food, so get going and put a move on.'

'Eeh by gum! Look at that!' Joe stopped in his slicing of the corned beef, and, sitting back on his heels, gazed upwards. 'The whole sky looks as if it's going to drop on us. And look at the funny colour ... It's getting darker. Coo!' He began with renewed vigour to slice up the remainder of the corned beef and slap it on to the bread.

Matty was now laying stones on the hessian flaps of the tent, and he said, 'If it doesn't come on to rain I'll make a can of tea on the Primus and take it in with us.'

When they had stacked everything they could in the back of their tent, cases, bedding, and food boxes, it looked as if there wasn't going to be any room for themselves; and after they had crawled in and got themselves arranged, Willie, on hands and knees, made his appearance at the open flap, and asked plaintively, 'Could I squeeze in?'

'Look at us, man.' Matty moved his hand over the congested space. 'We're packed.' He stared at Willie's long thin face, which was not smiling now, and which was only just discernible in the growing darkness, and, turning swiftly, he pushed Joe with an angry movement, saying, 'Bump the tins and cases out. He'll put them in his tent and that'll make the extra room ... We hope.'

'S'truth! Here we go again.'

There began another whirl of compressed activity as they rearranged themselves, and they were no sooner crouched in more or less comfortable positions than the heavens above them seemed to split open. The thunder was so terrific, so terrifying that even after its rumblings had become faint, they were still huddled together, faces pressed downwards, in the middle of the tent.

Matty was gasping as if he had been fighting against a strong wind. When he lifted his head he saw that it was almost like night now, and, following the noise of the thunder clap, so quiet as to be eerie. When neither of the others moved, he shook Joe, and then Willie, and whispered, 'You all right?'

'Eeh!' Joe's voice was trembling. 'That's what they call a thunderbolt, I suppose. Eeh! Man, I've never heard anything like it.' His voice was awe-filled.

As yet, Willie hadn't moved, and Matty shook him again, saying, 'You all right, Willie?'

Slowly Willie brought himself upwards, and the whiteness of his face seemed to shine through the dimness, and as Matty peered at him he realized that this big, overgrown pal of his, this laughter-making, joke-loving pal, was frightened. Well, that was nothing to be ashamed of; that bang had frightened him. But Willie's fright, he saw, was a different kind somehow; it was stark fear, more than temporary fright. Matty couldn't explain the difference to himself but it brought his hand on to Willie's shoulder as he said, 'Coo! That scared the daylights out of me.' He watched Willie's head make a little nod now, and he waited for him to speak. But he didn't.

'I could do with a drink of tea.' Matty touched Joe's arm. 'Hand the can over here; we'll have a sup all round.'

When Matty handed the can lid full of tea to Willie, he found he had to steady it before Willie could get a grip on it, and he thought again, It's funny a big fellow like him. But he did not despise his pal for his abject fear. In some, not quite under-standable, way he felt he had come to know Willie better in the last few minutes than ever before. It was all very puzzling.

The hot tea made them sweat, and Joe exclaimed, as he wiped his face with his hand, 'Eeh! I'm wringin'. I've never felt so hot in me life.'

'You hot, Willie?' Matty leant towards the quiet, dim figure.

'Aye . . . aye, Matty, I'm hot.'

'Once it starts to rain it'll get cooler. I wish it would hurry up; storms are not so bad if it rains.'

'I haven't seen any lightnin'.'

Joe had scarcely finished speaking when, as they all swore later, the lightning came straight through the tent. Certain it was that it not only illuminated the small space with a light, brighter than any sunshine, it also seemed to lift the tent, and themselves, from the ground, for it was accompanied within a split second by another terrific burst of thunder. Once again they were huddling together, and it was some longer time before they moved. When finally they came to disentangle themselves Matty found he had his arms about Willie, that Willie's face was buried somewhere near his side, and that they were both leaning over Joe.

'I'm scared. I don't mind tellin' you, I'm scared, Matty. Th . . . that was awful . . .'

Joe's admission of fear did not disturb Matty half as much as Willie's silence, his trembling silence now, for the boy's whole body was shaking. Matty's own voice had a tremor in it when he said, 'It'll be all right now. Listen. Here it comes . . . Hear it?' He lifted his head and looked up at the roof of the tent, so near to his face.

'It's wind,' said Joe.

'No, rain. I heard it like that once afore, the day when Mr Tollet took us on the fells. The storm came up just as we were going home and the rain sounded like wind coming from a distance, and he had to stop the car . . . There it is.'

As the first huge drops hit the canvas they all sighed with relief. It would be better now. Everybody knew that thunderstorms were soon over when it rained.

Whereas they had never experienced such thunder, or lightning, they were used to heavy rain. But within seconds they were made aware that this wasn't just rain; this was a force, a terrible force. All the clichés about raining cats and dogs, coming down in buckets, hailstones as big as marbles, a solid sheet of rain, seemed far short of an accurate description of this deluge that seemed bent on pressing them into the earth. The noise was such that if they had tried to speak they wouldn't have been heard.

Matty had pegged the tent flap in such a way as to leave a space to let the air in. Now, leaning forward, he groped wildly at the tape around the peg in an effort to shut the flap, but when once he had released it, it was torn from his hand. When he put his head out of the tent and grabbed at the wildly flapping canvas the rain stung his face like a hail of gravel.

The tent flap at last secure, he had pulled himself back into a sitting position, when Joe, nudging him hard in the ribs, thumbed the apex of the tent.

'Oh, no. No!' Willie groaned inwardly. They would be in a mess if the tent leaked.

It was evident in a very short space of time that they were in a mess. The tent was not only letting water in through the ridge, but it was coming in at the sides. Wherever their belongings touched the canvas there came a stream of water. Desperately, they drew their baggage and beds around them, and Matty and Joe struggled into their raincoats. Willie had a bicycle cape with him, and also a mack, but they were both in his tent. Matty, realizing this, pulled off his raincoat again and put half of it over Willie's head. He tried to laugh as he did so, but his effort was a failure, for it had no assistance from Willie. And so, huddled up, they sat in silent misery waiting for the storm to wear itself out, which, Matty reassured himself, couldn't be long. No storm, he imagined, could keep up this force for very long. He was to learn a lot within the next hour or so.

They were sitting in miserable dejection, the water pouring on them from all sides, the wind howling as they had never heard wind howl, and the thunder, although less violent, still crashing around them, when the main guy ropes snapped. In the deafening turmoil of the storm they didn't hear them go, but when the canvas suddenly collapsed about them they had all the evidence of their going that was needed.

Calling to each other, they disentangled themselves from the material that had taken on the weight of sailcloth, and, struggling blindly and soaked to the skin, they now fought their way to the dim outline of Willie's tent. And when, breathless, they collapsed together like sardines on top of bedding, tins and cases, they realized that their plight had not improved, for the rain was pouring straight through every pore in the little tent.

'What we going to do, man?' Although Joe was shouting into Matty's ear, his voice came like a tiny whisper; and Matty shouted back, 'It'll soon be over. It's bound to wear itself out.'

How much longer they lay in wet, abject misery Matty couldn't recall, but he was always to remember Mr Walsh's voice as it came from the mouth of the tent, bawling, 'Come on! Get out of that.' Music had never sounded more sweet to

Matty, nor had he seen a face so angelic as the hard, rock features of Mr Walsh peering from under the black brim of a sou'wester.

One after the other the farmer gripped them by their collars and pulled them to their feet, and steadying Joe with one arm, he waved wildly with the other, as he yelled, 'If your cases are dry, fetch them along.'

Going back into the tent, Matty grabbed up Willie's case and, pushing it into his hand, pointed to where the dim figures of Joe and Mr Walsh were moving slowly towards the gate. But Willie made no effort to go on his own; he stood waiting, hardly able to keep his feet, while Matty tore at his own collapsed tent and retrieved his case, and Joe's. With Joe's smaller case tucked under his arm, and carrying his own by the handle, he now put his free arm around Willie's shoulder. And Willie doing the same to him, they pressed their way blindly towards the gate. It was open, and they passed through without bothering to close it; this was no time to bother about gates, so Matty told himself.

When they entered the comparative shelter of the farmyard, the blurred figure of Mr Walsh came towards them and led them into the big barn, and around the tangle of machinery, to a great mound of dry straw. Had he walked into his mother's kitchen at this moment it could not have looked more home-like to Matty than that dry straw.

Joe was sitting on the edge of an upturned box and looked very small and dejected, like a little wet rat. He was still taking in great draughts of air, as were they all.

When Matty let go of Willie, Willie immediately sat down on the edge of the straw, only to be brought to his feet again by Mr Walsh saying quickly, 'Don't sit there in your wet things, if you're going to sleep on it. Look in your cases and see if your stuff is still dry and change your clothes right away. I'll bring you some blankets over.' Just before he turned away he said, 'And be careful of that lantern there.' He pointed to where a lantern was standing on the broad cross-beam of the barn wall. 'It's a safety one. But I wouldn't chance it being knocked over; so be careful.'

None of the boys made any answer. Not one of them had spoken since they came into the barn. They were too exhausted. And their movements, when they went to open their cases, were slow and laboured.

The contents of Matty's case were dry, and for this again he mentally thanked his mother. He had grumbled against taking the old battered leather suitcase because it was too heavy, but his clothes were as dry as when she had packed them. Willie's, too, were comparatively dry, but everything in Joe's thin composition case was wringing wet.

As Joe lifted one sodden garment out after another, Matty said, 'Well, never mind. Here's a shirt of mine; it'll do the night.'

'It'll reach to me feet, man.'

'Well, does that matter if you're lying down?'

'No, no.' Joe shook his head, and when he undressed and stood in Matty's shirt that fell around his ankles it did not drag a laugh from any of them.

Mr Walsh now came back into the barn. He was carrying a bulky bundle covered with a waterproof sheet, and behind him, dressed in oil-skins, like her husband, came Mrs Walsh, bearing

110

before her a large basket, like that which bakers carry bread in. As she set it on the ground, she said cheerily, 'Well, boys, that was a bit of a storm?'

It seemed to Matty not quite right when no one answered her, so he proffered, 'Yes. Yes, it was, Mrs Walsh.'

'It's set in; it'll likely go on for some time yet. But you'll come to no harm in here.' She took the cover off the basket, and, taking up a large pan, she began pouring steaming broth into three basins.

The bundle Mr Walsh had carried was of blankets. Handing them to the boys, he said, 'Here, roll yourselves in these and get into the straw there, and you'll think you're in an oven. And if you start sweating stay put; it'll get rid of any cold you've got.'

'Thanks, Mr Walsh.'

'Thanks, Mr Walsh.'

'Thanks, Mr Walsh.'

One after another, in docile voices, they thanked the farmer, then pulled the blankets around them and burrowed into the straw.

'You look like the three bears, sitting there.' Mr Walsh laughed as he took the bowls from his wife and handed them, first one to Matty, then to Willie, then to Joe. This was followed by great hunks of new bread and a spoon each.

Matty looked into the steaming broth; then towards Mrs Walsh, her face just discernible in the glow of the lamp and the shadow from her sou'wester hat, and he said softly, and with deep gratitude, 'Thank you, Mrs Walsh. It's more than good of you. Thank you.'

'That's all right. That's all right. And' – her voice went high in her head – 'don't you all look as if you had lost a sixpence and found a three-penny bit. Your stuff will dry out, and you'll see things differently in the daylight. It isn't the first time that campers have been washed out here in a storm. Is it, Arthur?'

'No, not by a long chalk. You're not the first, and you won't be the last. Take your time over that broth, and I'll come back later and put the light out. Put the basins to the side there, then get yourselves off to sleep. Good-night to you.'

'Good-night, Mr Walsh. Good-night, Mrs Walsh.' Their voices were louder now, more normal sounding, and when the farmer and his wife had departed they drank greedily at the soup. Then Joe, giving a big sigh, exclaimed, 'Eeh! I'll never forget this night as long as I live. Things might look better in the morning, as Mrs Walsh says, but still I'll not forget this night.'

Willie didn't add his usual laughing quip to this remark, but Matty said, 'I don't think any of us will forget it. To tell the truth, it had me scared.'

'Scared?' said Joe. 'That's putting it mildly for me. Were you scared, Willie?'

'Oh! Aye. Aye, I was.'

As Matty listened to this admission he knew it referred to the normal scaring storms created in most people, but he was aware that his pal was still trying to press down the fear that had run wild in him when he had been out there on the open hillside. To say that Willie had been as frightened of the storm as any hysterical girl sounded unbelievable, but, Matty knew, it was nevertheless true. He recalled at this moment that his grandmother had been petrified of spiders until the day she died, and his mother saying to him one day, 'All folks have their private

112

fears.' He hadn't understood what she meant then, but he did now.

He finished his soup and the last mouthful of bread and exclaimed brightly, 'By, that feels better. What about you, Joe?'

'Me? I feel a new man.'

'Well, let's get down; we don't want to be jabbering when Mr Walsh comes back ... Are you finished, Willie?'

'Aye.' Willie put the basin down to the side of him.

'How are you feelin'?'

'Me?' said Willie. 'Oh! I'm feelin' fine now. But lord! I was cold out there. After all that heat the day I never thought I'd be cold again, but you know, man, I was shiverin' just as if it were winter.'

'And it's not far off, if you ask me,' said Matty. 'As for cold, my teeth were going like castanets.' He paused and wriggled his hips deep into the straw. 'Well, here's me for dreamland.'

As they settled down there was no joking. The terror of the storm was still too recent.

Matty was dragged up out of deep, warm comfort by a voice seeming to bawl through his head, crying, 'Come on with you! You going to sleep all day?'

As he dragged himself upwards he saw Joe and Willie already sitting up, both rubbing the sleep out of their eyes.

'There's a can of tea for you, and there's a pump in the yard. Get yourselves up and get a wash. Then get over and clear up the shambles. And let me tell you, if it wasn't that you're an inexperienced lot, and were hard put to it in the storm, I'd feel inclined to use me boot on you this morning. At least one of you. Who was last through that gate last night?'

Mr Walsh's voice still seemed to be bawling through Matty's dazed mind. Who was last through the gate? he was asking himself. He and Willie came last through the gate, but Willie had been in no shape to think about shutting the gate. Neither had he for that matter. He squinted up at Mr Walsh, and said, 'I was, I suppose.'

'You suppose! You were or you weren't?'

The farmer's tone brought Matty into full wakefulness. It also brought a snapping retort to his tongue, which he had the good sense to check; he said quietly, 'It was me.'

'Aye, I thought it was. Well now, as I said, I'm making allowances, but don't let it happen again. I let the pigs out sometimes in the morning to run around, and if I hadn't gone round that way and seen the gate open you would have had more than wet canvas to deal with this morning, me lads. Well now, up you get and have this tea and get busy.'

The three of them looked at Mr Walsh's back as he went down the barn, walking in between the machinery, but no comment was made. Then yawning, and stretching, and grunting, they disentangled themselves from their blankets, and their warm nest.

As Joe finished his mug of tea he pointed towards the doorway and said in surprise, 'Look! The sun's shining. After last night, the sun's shining.'

The sun recalled to Joe the condition of his clothes, and now he said dolefully, 'What am I going to put on? I haven't a dry rag.'

'Well, keep that shirt on,' said Matty, 'and you can have my other shorts.'

'Eeh! but, man, they'll come down to me heels.'

'Well,' said Matty with seeming indifference, 'don't wear any at all; it's up to you.' As he said this he pulled the shorts from his case and threw them towards Joe. The next minute he was trying to smother his laughter as he looked at Joe. The shirt sleeves trailed far below his hands, and the outsize shorts came well below his calves.

'Eeh! I'll look a pickle.'

'You've said it.' Willie looked, and sounded, his own bright self this morning. 'You'd get a prize in the carnival if you went in like that.'

'Aw, look, man, I can't go outside like this.'

'Well,' said Matty, 'as I said, it's up to you. You can stay here all day. But I'm going to have a wash. Then I'm going over to see if I can cook some breakfast.'

As Willie, still laughing, followed Matty, Joe brought up the rear, protesting loudly, and after they had sluiced their faces under the pump and dried themselves on the coarse towel hanging over a rail, they returned to the barn, folded the blankets and put them in a pile. Then Matty said, 'I'll have to take these back.'

'I'll take them, if you like,' volunteered Willie, a twisted smile on his face. 'Aw no, you won't,' said Matty. 'If you take these, you'll land yourself inside for breakfast, and we'll be left out in the cold, cold snow.'

It wasn't Willie who answered Matty now but Joe, and he screwed up his face as he said slowly, 'You know, you're funny, Matty.'

'Funny?' Matty narrowed his eyes at him over the top of the blankets.

'Aye, sort of. You're so sure you wouldn't be invited in for breakfast.'

'Aye, I am.' Matty now strode on ahead and

115

went down the farmyard and turned off to the left, and to the kitchen door. And there he was met by Mrs Walsh.

'By, you've soon got moving.' She took the blankets from Matty and put them on a table just inside the door, saying, 'I'll put them out in the sun later. Who knows but you'll need them tonight again.'

'I hope not, Mrs Walsh.'

'It was a bad storm, one of the worst we've had for some time. But you get all kinds of weather and you get used to dealing with it.'

'It seemed different to other thunderstorms I've heard,' said Matty.

'That's because you're closed in in the town. Here, in the open, there seems so much more of it.'

'Aye, you're right. There seemed a lot of it last night.'

She smiled broadly at him. 'Anyway, the sun's hot again and it'll soon dry your things out.'

'Thanks for the blankets . . . and the tea, Mrs Walsh.'

'You're very welcome, boy, you're very welcome.'

When Matty joined Willie, who was alone now, Joe having scurried on ahead in case he was seen, Willie said briefly, 'No invitation?'

'No invitation,' said Matty. 'I told you.'

'By, I'm hungry,' said Willie.

'Well, the Primus will be all right; we'll soon get something goin' on that. And the bread was in the biscuit tin, and that should be all right.'

When they came to the encampment, Joe was standing looking about him in dismay. The wrecked tent, like a piece of old wet rag, lay flat on the ground, secured only by one rope. On the patch of ground it had covered lay a sodden jumble of bedding, tins and knapsacks.

Surprisingly, Willie's tent was still erect, and when they felt the canvas it was almost dry.

'Come on!' said Matty briskly. 'You light that Primus, Joe, and get some water boiling. You, Willie; help me strip the sleeping bags. We'll hang them over the wall. We'll put everything on the wall; it'll catch the sun better there . . .'

It was half-an-hour later, when everything was spread out on the wall and Joe had just managed to make a pot of tea that Jessica came hurrying into the field. She was carrying what looked like a small covered dish. As they stopped what they were doing and watched her approach, their mouths began to water, for the smell of bacon preceded her. 'My mother thought you mightn't be able to get your fire going with the wood being wet; she sent you these bacon sandwiches.' She balanced the dish on one hand and raised the lid, and watched their faces brighten.

'Oh! Thanks. Thank your mother, will you?' Matty took the dish from her. 'It's good of her.'

'Aye, it's good of her,' Joe endorsed.

'When I win the sweep I'll buy her a first-rate cooker,' said Willie.

'She's got one. She wouldn't cook on anything but our stove if she'd got a million. She always says so.'

'So you can keep your cooker.' Joe nodded at Willie, and they all laughed.

'Be seeing you.' They watched her for a moment running across the field, her hair flying out behind her. Then, simultaneously, they attacked the dish, and as they ate ravenously they each said, in his own way, that they had

117

never tasted anything like the new bread, or the thick slices of home-cured bacon.

It was around eleven in the morning when Mr Walsh, accompanied by Jessica, paid them a visit. Would they, he wanted to know, like to come and see the dogs at work? Before the others could even think of a reply, Matty exclaimed excitedly, 'Oh yes, please. I'd love that.'

'But what about the things?' put in Joe. 'They're not dry yet. And what if it comes on to rain?'

'Oh, it won't rain until we get back. I can assure you of that,' said Mr Walsh.

'Well, I'm not going,' said Jessica, 'so if it starts to spot I can get them down for you . . .'

Before she had finished speaking Willie put in, stammering now, 'O-oh, there's no ne . . . need because I c . . . can't do a long trek. Not with me heel. It isn't quite better yet. You two go on.'

There was a quick exchange of glances between Joe and Matty. Then Mr Walsh said in his impatient way, 'Well, come on, whoever's coming. Get your boots on; we want no more sore heels.'

Joe was now wearing his own shorts, which were more or less dry, but when, after pulling off his plimsolls, he tried to get into his shoes he found they were still soaking wet, and most uncomfortable. 'You can't walk far in those,' said Mr Walsh, looking down on him as he struggled to push a stockinged foot into the shoes. 'That's you out an' all. What about you?' Mr Walsh had turned to Matty.

'Oh, these boots are all right, Mr Walsh; I had them in me case.'

'Well, let's get going.' Mr Walsh led the way, and Matty, after one quizzical look at Willie, and a quick wink at Joe, hurried after the farmer.

Matty came up with Mr Walsh at the gate, and he dropped into step with him but did not speak. Nor did Mr Walsh open a conversation, but what he did was to whistle. It was a long, low sustained note. They had passed the farm and were on the road that was new to Matty when he saw the answer to Mr Walsh's call, for there, bounding down the foothills beyond the farm, came racing the two dogs. After they had circled their master and Matty once, Betsy, taking the lead, fell in just behind Mr Walsh, walking to his left heel, while Prince came just behind her.

Matty kept glancing back towards the two dogs, and it was when Betsy veered away from her master's side just a trifle that Mr Walsh growled, 'Steady. Steady.' Then without looking at Matty he said, 'Don't do that. Never try to distract a dog's attention from its work.'

When they reached a path where the ground levelled out before rising again, Mr Walsh stopped, and the dogs slowly lowered themselves to the grass and sat with tongues lolling, while Matty stood looking around him in awed wonder. Then more to himself than to the farmer, he said, 'I didn't know there were so many hills in the world.'

'Don't insult them, lad; they don't like to be called hills; they like to be called mountains, or rocks.'

'Rocks?' repeated Matty.

'Aye, mud rocks ... slate rocks ... volcanic rocks. Skiddaw, the Newlands Fells, and the fells about Whinlatter Pass are all slate. And there are many others. These, they say, were left by the sea. Then there are the Scafell rocks under the Coniston and the Helvellyn range. These, they

119

say, are the result of volcanoes, and some of the volcanic slates are green.'

'Green!' said Matty questioningly. 'With grass?'

'No. No. Just green . . . And see. Right over there towards the coast, you cannot see it from here, lies Coniston. Have you heard of Shap granite?'

Matty shook his head.

'They make street flags with it. Some of London is paved with it, they tell me. It's a fine sight to see it in its natural setting, layer upon layer of natural white limestone. But you've got to go to the Pennines to see that . . . Well, come on.' He turned abruptly. 'My sheep know nothing about mud rocks or Shap granite, they only know about grass. And you'll see grass up here as smooth as a cat's back.'

They were climbing again . . . up . . . up . . . up to the top of the world Matty thought, and although he was hot, even sweating, he realized that the air was cooler here. At one point, he saw a great shining stretch of water, but he hadn't the breath to ask Mr Walsh which lake it was, for they were going down the other side of the mountain now, and Mr Walsh was skipping like a young boy down the narrow twisting path.

When they were at last on comparatively level ground, Matty saw before him a long funnel-like valley with gentle slopes rising at each side of it. But to the immediate right of them lay a wide expanse of green, and dotting it like buttons were a large number of black-faced sheep.

And now Matty saw, and heard, what to him was an amazing thing, Mr Walsh giving orders to Betsy, and she obeying them implicitly. First, the farmer pointed his stick in the direction of a path that seemed to lead around the foot of the mountain they had just come over, and said, 'Away, girl.'

As Betsy streaked towards the sheep, Prince now moved up close to Mr Walsh's side. The dog's whole body was visibly trembling, and Mr Walsh, without looking at him, said sharply, 'Steady, boy. Wait.'

Betsy was now rounding the herd, running, then dropping on all fours; waiting; then up again. When one sheep slipped from the group the dog was after it and brought it into line, and for the first time Matty heard her bark, just one sharp bark, like an order.

Matty was following Mr Walsh and Prince now, but keeping a distance behind him in case he inadvertently did something to distract the dog. Matty never heard the farmer's order to the younger dog, but he saw it suddenly streak away to the flank of the close-packed moving sheep.

Mr Walsh now whistled again, and this brought the two dogs to a dead stop. It also halted the sheep; and with leisurely, but measured tread, the farmer went round the foot of a hill, and going towards a roughly made gate he lifted it off its hinges, placed it against the wall, then moved a short distance away, before giving another order to the dogs.

Within minutes the sheep were all through the gap and into the next field. At least, Matty thought it was a field, until he was at the other side of the dry stone wall. Then he saw it was just another great stretch of low fells.

The dogs did not keep to heel, but frolicked here and there along the path. And when the older dog came bounding back, and right to Matty's legs, he put his hand down swiftly and

121

patted its head. But when Betsy stayed at his side, as he made his way behind Mr Walsh, he became uneasy, in case of another reprimand.

They were returning to the farm by a different, and not half so arduous, way as that by which they had come. During the journey Matty found the silence something of a test, but it wasn't in him to open a conversation. It wasn't until the farm came almost into view that Mr Walsh said abruptly, 'What are you going into?'

'Going into?' repeated Matty hastily. 'You mean . . .?'

'I mean, what are you going to work at?' Mr Walsh's voice sounded high, and impatient, and this caused Matty's reply to become stilted. 'The docks.'

'Why are you going in the docks?'

'Well.' He hesitated; then went on slowly, 'That's all I can do. And me dad wants me to go in.'

'The others tell me they're going to be apprenticed; why couldn't you do the same?'

Not for the life of him could Matty tell the farmer the truth, and say, I don't want to go in the docks, not in any capacity, I want to work with animals, because, he imagined, it would bring a hoot of derision from this brusque man. Didn't every boy who visited a farm say he wanted to become a farmer? This desire was too near to him, too real, too painful to stand derision of any kind, without causing him to lose his temper. And he was well aware that it wouldn't pay anyone to lose their temper with a man like Mr Walsh.

'Aye. Well, you know where the money lies and I suppose that counts for something these days. You can't have it all ways. Well now, have you enjoyed what you've seen?'

'Oh, yes. Yes.' Somehow Matty couldn't get

into his voice the enthusiasm which he felt. He had been thrilled and excited with the journey over the mountain, and he realized now, since they had come back this comparatively easy way, that the farmer had purposely taken the stiff climb to reach the far valley simply to point out the magnificence of the hills . . . or rocks. Oh aye! Matty smiled to himself. He mustn't forget that the big ones didn't like to be called hills.

This touch of humour coming into his thinking, decided Matty that he must in some way convey the pleasure he had experienced during the past two hours to Mr Walsh. The decision made, the words gathered swiftly in his mouth, and he was actually about to open the conversation, when the farmer, pointing to a stone wall around which they were walking, said, 'If you jump that and cross the field you'll come to your camp behind the next wall.'

Matty paused, then stopped. The spontaneity sank in him. 'Thanks. Thanks, Mr Walsh. I . . . I've enjoyed it.' Again he sounded hesitant.

Mr Walsh slanted his glance towards him, a half smile on his face. Then saying, 'I . . . I believe you, lad,' he strode away, leaving Matty knowing full well that he didn't believe him, and feeling that he wanted to punch himself for not being able to convince the farmer of the truth of his statement.

When he reached the wall he was surprised to see his two pals sitting aimlessly whittling pieces of wood, and as he jumped the wall they got to their feet immediately and questioned him about his walk.

'Oh, it was fine, fine. Hard going at first.' His voice sounded airy. 'Boy, didn't we climb! But it was worth it, man. I've never seen anything like it. We'll have to go there afore we go home.' He looked from one to the other, then asked, 'What's the matter with you two?'

'Nowt,' said Willie quickly.

But Joe, his head lowered, said, 'We're a bit fed up.'

'Fed up?' Matty's jaw actually dropped. 'What you fed up about? We've hardly got here. We've done nothing yet.'

'That's it,' said Willie. 'You can't get anywhere unless you walk miles.'

'Well, we can take the bus. We were going to Blanchland today, and round about there, weren't we?'

'Aye.' Willie nodded slowly. 'But you've got to walk all down that blooming road, then back up. It took us forty minutes the other mornin'. That's when we were fresh. And Jessica says the bus only passes the bottom every two hours.'

'But we didn't come to use buses, we came to camp, and walk.' Matty thrust his head out towards Willie now.

'Oh, aye, man, I know. I was just sayin'. But anyway, Joe thinks like me. Don't you, Joe?'

'I do a bit, Matty.' Joe looked shamefaced as he made this statement. 'There isn't much to do.'

Matty sat slowly down on a large stone. He was deeply perplexed. The others sat down, and after an uncomfortable silence, Joe said, 'We were goin' for a walk. Jessica was goin' to take us down to the part where you can swim . . . show us the easiest way to get there, then her mother came for her. Do you know somethin', Matty? She's clever. Isn't she, Willie?'

Willie merely nodded to this. And Joe went on, 'She told us all about a writer called Beatrix Potter, who lived round here, a place called Coniston, on a farm the name of ... Eeh. Eeh, I've forgotten.'

'Tilberthwaite Farm,' put in Matty quickly. 'Aye, I know all about Beatrix Potter.'

'Oh!' Joe raised his eyebrows. Then not to be outdone, he went on, 'She was learning us to count in a different language; her grandfather used to count like it. Yan, tan, tether. What's the other, Willie? How does it go?'

'Pimp something,' said Willie.

'No, pimp is five, I know that. She said it's Scandinavian counting.'

'Why didn't you go on and find the pool by yourselves?' said Matty now.

'Oh!' Willie jerked his head backwards. 'There seemed no point, man. We've seen the stream, it all looks alike.'

'Oh, godfathers!' Matty punched his brow with his closed fist. 'You've seen nothing yet. I tell you we've just come; we've hardly settled in.'

'Well,' said Joe, getting to his feet quickly, 'don't get your rag out, Matty. Let's get some grub up and then go to that Blanchland place.'

After a moment Matty got to his feet and set about getting the meal ready, but he did it silently, for he was disturbed. They had come on Saturday, and this was Tuesday of the first week, and his pals were bored. He couldn't understand it; he just couldn't understand it.

7

By the time Saturday came around it had become absolutely plain to Matty that the camping holiday was not a success. Willie and Joe had had enough. They both agreed that camping would have been fine if the farm had been near a town, or a village where there were houses to look at, and people to see, but this wild, isolated spot held no attraction for them in any form.

It was Willie who actually proposed breaking up the camp and returning home. On Thursday he had said what was the good of staying on if the weather was going to change. It had been dull on Thursday. But Friday had been gloriously warm. Now it was bright and warm too, but Joe and Willie, sitting on the bank of the stream idly aiming pebbles at a jutting rock were talking about, of all things, the splendours of their home town. Never before had they realized that South Shields was such a wonderful place, and never had two boys more wholeheartedly longed to be back in its bustling work-a-day world.

But next minute everything changed as Mr Walsh, with pipe in mouth, and the dogs at his heels, came round the hill and shouted to them, 'We're away into town. Anybody like to take the trip into Hexham?'

'Oh, yes! Yes!' Joe and Willie were scrambling

towards him. Matty came up more slowly.

'Well then, get yourselves ready, and be quick about it. I'll be there all day, mind.'

'Oh, it suits us,' cried Willie, excited now as he raced up the field.

Mr Walsh was standing looking at Matty now, and he said one word to him, 'Well?' It had a big question mark attached to it, and Matty said, 'If you don't mind, I'd rather stay here.'

'Please yourself. Please yourself.' Mr Walsh glanced away quickly then asked, 'You broke?'

'Oh no! No. I've got a couple of quid left.' He smiled now. 'It's just that I don't want to go into the town; I'll have enough of it next week.'

Mr Walsh looked back at him appraisingly. 'You're a funny boy,' he said, and on this he turned abruptly away and left Matty standing staring after him.

Ten minutes later, Matty, standing beside Mrs Walsh, watched Jessica climb up into the cab beside her father, then his pals get into the back of the lorry. He watched Mr Walsh securing the bolts in the back flap; he watched him kiss his wife – a slight embarrassment this, for he had never seen his dad kiss his mother – then, when the lorry started up, they all waved back and forth to each other until it disappeared from view.

'Well, there now.' Mrs Walsh drew in a deep breath, then said, 'What are you going to do with yourself?'

'Oh, just knock about. I'll go for a tramp this afternoon.'

She nodded at him, saying, 'Yes, you want to take advantage of the weather when it's fine.'

'Mrs Walsh.' He paused. 'Do you think I could take the dogs with me? Or one of them?'

'Yes. Yes, of course. They would love it.'

'Oh, thanks.' He jerked his head at her, then asked hastily, 'Is . . . is there anything I can do for you? I mean on the farm.'

'No, I don't think so. I think Mr Walsh saw to everything before he left.'

'What I meant was, mucking anything out, like turning the manure again.'

Mrs Walsh laughed now, a high pleasant laugh, and she said teasingly, 'You don't want to turn the manure. Now, do you?'

'Oh.' Matty's face was quite straight. 'Oh, Mrs Walsh, I don't mind, not really. I quite liked doing it.'

She was staring at him, her own face straight. Then she said softly, 'I think you mean it.'

'I do, Mrs Walsh. I'd help swill the cow byres out. Or anything.' He became bold now. 'Who has to do it when Mr Walsh is away? You?'

'Yes. Who else? The cows must be milked, and there's only the two of us.'

'Well then, there's bound to be jobs I can do.'

'But I thought you wanted to go for a walk.'

'Oh, that was only to fill in the time.' He was smiling now, and she was smiling. 'Come and have a cup of coffee with me, and then we'll get going,' she said.

For many years after Matty was to remember his first real day on the farm, and as he inhaled the different smells, some sweet, and some far from sweet, he told himself that he was storing them up against his first day in the docks.

He spent an hour on the manure heap, then cleaned out the pigs; then, on an invitation to take 'a bite to eat' with Mrs Walsh, he cleaned himself up, and as he sat at the corner of the white scrubbed kitchen table, partly covered with a cloth, and ate his first real meal since he left home, he experienced a new pleasure. He couldn't put a name to it; it was just that he felt sort of happy in this kitchen, and strangely at ease sitting opposite this compact, nice looking little woman.

The feeling of comfort stayed with him all afternoon as he fetched and carried while Mrs Walsh did the milking, as he unfastened the cows from their boxes and watched them one after the other go out into the yard and make their way back to the field. After this he hosed the byres down, and playfully rubbed at each little name-plate attached to the supporting posts: Dolly, Jean, Maisie, Kitty, Bett, Rosie and Lulu. He laughed at the last name. Fancy calling a cow Lulu. And already he could distinguish Lulu from the rest of them, for she was frisky, and inclined to use her back legs. And so the afternoon passed, one pleasure adding to another, not the least of them when he sat down once again opposite Mrs Walsh to a wonderful tea of new bread, thick butter and home-made jam, and, added to this, dollops of fresh cream.

When, at half-past six, the sun disappeared and a mist came rolling in from the hills, he ran to the camp and quickly got the bedding from the wall and into the tents. He had just finished doing this when he heard the lorry stopping at the gate. The next minute Willie and Joe were in the field, yelling their greeting to him. They came up, both talking at once.

'Eeh! You should have come, man. It was grand. We went everywhere. Hexham is grand. The market an' all. And we went to the pictures.'

'The pictures?'

'Well, Jessica doesn't often get to the pictures,

and she said she would like to go. And her dad said it was all right, and he picked us up after and gave us a tea. Didn't he, Joe?'

'Aye.' Joe nodded quickly. 'A slap up one, an' all. I had sausage and eggs, and Willie had fish and chips ... What have you been doin' with yourself?'

'Oh, just knockin' about.' Matty smiled.

'Did you go for a walk?' asked Willie.

'No.' Matty shook his head. 'I've been on the farm all day, doing bits here and there.'

'Not on the muck heap?' Joe laughed.

'Aye. Yes, I did an hour on there.'

'You're barmy ... Here!' Willie threw a paper bag towards him, and when Matty caught it and opened it, and saw three sticks of chewing gum, a Mars bar, a Crunchie, and a slab of toffee, he looked at Willie and, grinning widely, said, 'Thanks, man.'

'We bought it atween us,' said Joe.

'Thanks, Joe.'

'An' look. I bought this for me mother.' Joe held out a card, to which was pinned a glittering brooch.

'That's nice,' said Matty.

'Paid four-and-six for it.'

'Go on. It looks worth more than that.'

'Aye. That's what I thought.'

'Coo! I'm hungry.' Willie looked towards the fireplace.

'But I thought you said you'd had your tea?'

'That's ages ago, man. Let's have a cook-up. I bought some sausage and black and white puddin'.'

'An' we've got some brawn for the morrow, and pigs' trotters,' put in Joe. 'Eeh! them trotters.' Joe covered his face with his hands. 'Do you know what Willie said when we bought the trotters and the man said is there anything more you want? Do you know what he said? Eeh! and the way he said it.' Joe could hardly go on for laughing. 'When the man said, "Is there anything else you want?" he said, "Aye, the pig that went with the trotters. Where you hidin' him? Come on now, where you hidin' him?" You should have seen the man's face. He didn't think it was funny.'

They were all laughing now and they laughed as they cooked the meal. Later, even from their sleeping bags they went on laughing. It had been a grand day for all of them.

But Sunday brought dullness in the weather and dullness of spirits. After the chores were done Willie took on the self-appointed task of going to the farm for the milk; but he was soon back, Mr Walsh having given him the milk, as Mrs Walsh had gone down to Slaggyford to see her brother who was still ill. Jessica had gone with her. So Willie lay in his tent most of the morning, and only under protest did he don a mack and go for a walk in the afternoon. Most of the time he discussed with Joe the plot of the picture they had seen the day before.

Monday the sun shone, but the weather was cool. They went down to the stream and threw pebbles, and it was while they were sitting on the bank that Betsy paid them a visit. But it was evident from the beginning that the dog had come to see one person only, for when she could disengage herself from the patting and stroking of Willie and Joe, she settled herself down by Matty's side, and Matty, putting his arm about her, gently pressed her to him.

131

'It's funny about dogs and you,' said Joe; 'they always make for you.'

'It's his bark,' said Willie; 'he's nearly one of them.'

This was a reference to an altercation Willie and Matty had had earlier over half-washed pans. Willie had left as much dirt on the inside of the pans as was on the outside by the time he had finished with them and Matty had gone for him. But now Matty did not take it up. He went on fondling the dog, content because Betsy had singled him out.

The boredom reached its height that evening when a drizzle set in. For a time the three of them sat crushed together in the tent and exhausted their repertoire of songs, Willie accompanying in a sketchy fashion on his mouth organ. But when the time came to go out into the drizzle and coax the fire, or wait for the slow process of the Primus if they wanted a drink, Willie suddenly exclaimed, 'Aw, man, I've had a bellyful. Come on, Matty; let's go home the morrow.'

'Look, Willie.' Matty kept his voice low but his tone was definite as he said, 'You can do as you like, but me, I'm staying until Saturday. This holiday is goin' to have to last me a long time, and I'm making the most of it.'

'You call it a holiday? I don't understand you, man. We've done nothing but loaf about.'

'That's your fault.' Matty shook his head at him. But still keeping his tone low, he went on, 'Now tomorrow, whether you like it or not, and whether it's rain or shine, I'm going for a long tramp.' He turned to Joe now. 'What d'you say, Joe?'

'Well.' Joe pulled his knees up and leant his elbows on them. Then looking down, he said,

'I think Willie's right, Matty. I can't help it.'

As Matty looked at his pal he felt no anger, only a touch of sadness, and a keen sense of disappointment. 'I thought you were looking forward to going to Hexham with Mr Walsh again,' he said quietly.

'Aye, but that isn't until Wednesday.'

Matty got slowly up and went out of the tent. He brought some dried wood he had left under cover and, putting it on the still hot embers, he gradually blew them into a blaze. He made the cocoa and took the steaming mugs into the tent, and apart from Joe and Willie saying 'Ta', there was no exchange of any kind.

They were all in their sleeping bags before it was quite dark, and, except for muttered goodnights, they had nothing to say to each other. As Matty lay staring upwards, he knew that the other two weren't asleep. Joe made this evident by tossing and turning, and there was a sound of distant rustling from Willie's tent.

Then, at the same instant he and Joe were sitting up peering at each other as they heard Mr Walsh's voice shouting from a distance, 'Hi, there!'

Matty, pulling himself out of his bag, scrambled on hands and knees to the tent flap and stuck his head out, there to see Willie in the same position.

'Do you want us, Mr Walsh?' called Matty.

'Yes, I want you.' The voice was nearer now. 'What did I tell you about shutting gates?'

'I've never left the gate open,' said Matty under his breath, turning his head to Joe who was at his side now.

'Come along here and close it.'

'But we're in bed, Mr Walsh.' It was Willie

who answered the farmer, and Mr Walsh's voice came rapping back at him, 'Well, get out of bed and come and close this gate. That'll teach you a lesson.'

Matty scrambled into his boots and tucked the tops of his pyjama legs into them; then grabbing up his waterproof mack that was lying by his bed, he pulled it on as he went out into the darkness.

The dim outline of Mr Walsh was visible now and his voice came at Matty harsh and angry. 'I told you, didn't I, about the gate. I made a point of it.'

'But I closed the gate, Mr Walsh. It wasn't me.'

'I don't care who it was. You're responsible and you should see to these things last thing at night before you turn in. Now you can take a trip and close it after I've gone out. That'll teach you a lesson.' At this he stalked away, and Matty followed him slowly, guided by his angry voice, saying, 'I stopped letting the field years ago, and I'll do it again. I told you about the pigs first thing in the morning. Scatter-brained, the lot of you; no sense of responsibility.'

When Matty reached the gate it was wide open. He lifted it into place and slipped the steel spoke through the chain, then stood, for a moment, listening to Mr Walsh's footstep fading away as he went towards the farm. He felt mad with the farmer. Every time he had used the gate he had seen it was firmly closed. Yet it didn't matter who left the gate open, as Mr Walsh had said, he was going to be held responsible. It wasn't fair. It was bloomin' unjust, and that was putting it mildly.

He was shivering with cold when he got back to his tent, and he didn't speak until he was in the warmth of his sleeping bag. Then, sitting up and holding the bag under his chin to try and prevent his teeth chattering, he shouted to Willie, 'Do you know anything about that gate?' There was a pause before Willie replied briefly, 'I shut it.'

'You couldn't have shut it. It wouldn't swing open on its own. Why couldn't you have owned up instead of letting me carry the can?'

'Aw, I'm fed up. This is the finish. I'm off in the mornin' and that's final.'

'Good enough! Good enough!' Matty was bawling now, and as he lay down he turned his head in Joe's direction and added, 'That goes for you and all.'

8

But Willie and Joe didn't go home the following day. They fully intended to when they got up in the morning. The intention was still firm as they sulkily ate their breakfast, but it was just as they were finishing the meal that they saw, walking towards them, from the direction of the stream, a familiar figure, yet one so unexpected in this place that they all thought they were seeing things.

So did Mr Funnell, for when he was some yards from them, he stopped and exclaimed, 'Well! I never.'

'Mr Funnell. You! Fancy seeing you here.' They crowded round him. 'And fancy seeing *you* here,' he answered. 'I didn't know you went camping.'

'Where've you come from, so early, sir?' asked Willie.

'Oh, I spent the night in Lambley. But I've been on the road since six.'

'But there's no road down there.' Joe was pointing towards the stream.

'Isn't there?' Mr Funnell bent down to him. 'There's roads everywhere, if you know them. I know this district well.'

'You do, sir . . .? And Mr Walsh?'

'Oh, Mr Walsh is an old friend of mine. I'm making for there now.'

'What d'you know?' Joe was shaking his head.

136

Then he asked hastily, 'Would you like a cup of tea, sir?'

'I would that,' said Mr Funnell readily. 'I haven't had a drink since half-past five.' He loosened his rucksack from his back and sat down on a stone. Then looking around him, he said, 'You're well organized I see. Proper fireplace, grease pit, nice little kitchen. Well! Well!' He now looked from one to another. 'I'm very glad to see you doing this. Have you enjoyed it?'

On this question Willie and Joe had the grace to look sheepish, and Willie bent his head a little as he said, 'Well, sir, it's a bit different from Shields.'

'I should hope so,' said Mr Funnell. 'That's why you came here. Don't tell me you've been bored.' He was looking at Joe now. And Joe grinned engagingly back at the master as he answered, 'Just a bit, sir. It would be marvellous if we were near a town.'

'Ooh!' It was a long-drawn-out sound. 'If you were near a town.' Mr Funnell shook his head slowly. 'And what about you, Doolin?'

'Oh, I've enjoyed it, sir, every minute. I don't want to go back.' Matty now handed the master a cup of tea and asked, 'Do you take sugar, sir?'

'Three big ones. More if you can spare it.' They all laughed.

Then, after Mr Funnell had drunk deeply from the mug, he said, 'How have you got on with Mr Walsh?'

'Aw.' Both Willie and Joe made the sound together. 'He can be a tartar at times.'

Mr Funnell's head was back and he was laughing heartily. 'Oh! Then you haven't been behaving yourselves?'

'Yes, we have, but . . . but Willie left the gate

open last night and Mr Walsh got us up in the dark. At least he did Matty. He made him get up and close it.' Joe nodded towards Matty, and Mr Funnell said, 'Oh, well. It's a serious offence, leaving a gate open, you know. He's got a quick temper has Mr Walsh, but he's a good man.' He jerked his chin up and repeated, 'A good man. You could learn a lot from him, if you liked.'

'Aw, we've left school, sir.' This quip came from Joe, and Mr Funnell said, 'So you've got no need to learn any more?'

'No, sir.'

The master shook his head slowly, but there was a smile on his face. Then rising to his feet, he said, 'Well I'm going to sample, at least I hope I am . . . one of Mrs Walsh's amazing breakfasts. But I'll be seeing you. I'll come over after and have a natter. Thanks for the tea.'

He took a few steps from them, then turned and said, 'I still can't get over the surprise of seeing you all here. I don't think I'll ever get over it.' He seemed to be addressing Willie and Joe rather than Matty. And Willie said, 'And we've had a shock an' all, sir.'

'Oh, I do this route every year without fail. If I don't see you before, and you come next year, we're sure to meet up.'

When he was out of earshot Willie said, 'Not likely. You'll not get me here next year, or any other time.' Then turning to Matty, he said quite cheerily, 'But didn't you get a surprise? Eeh? I thought I was seeing things.'

'Yes, I did an' all,' said Matty.

'He's a nice bloke, is Funnell.' Joe went to the frying pan and, with a piece of bread, rubbed it dry, and as he ate he looked sideways at Willie, saying, 'We can't go the day if he's here.'

'No, likely not. Mr Walsh won't take our kit down to the station if he's got a visitor.'

Matty, in his tent now and getting his things ready for airing, smiled to himself. They had made their point; they were staying on. The next minute he was disturbed by the thought that he was disappointed that they were staying, and he imagined what it would have been like if Mr Funnell had happened to call in when he was here on his own. Perhaps under those circumstances the master would have asked him to accompany him on a tramp. He would have liked that. Oh aye. He would have liked that. But as things were it wasn't likely there would be such an invitation thrown his way.

But Matty was wrong in this; there was an invitation thrown his way, and by Mr Funnell. The only snag was it included Willie and Joe, who grabbed at it as if their one pleasure in life was hiking. When Willie, in particular, showed intensified excitement at the fact that Mr Walsh and Jessica were going to join the party, Matty thought everyone would be justified in thinking that he himself was barmy were he to tell them that these two pals of his were fed up with walking uphill and down dales, were sick of the sight of mountains, and never wanted to see the country again, or anyone belonging to it, as long as they lived.

But now they were taking the same path over the mountain that Matty and Mr Walsh had taken a few days earlier. And on seeing it for the second time Matty was finding the scenery even more wonderful than before.

'There you are, Stanley. Does it look any

different?' Mr Walsh had stopped, and was pointing from the high promontory across the valley.

It was odd to hear Mr Funnell addressed as Stanley, and it brought Matty's attention away from the awe-inspiring view and made him smile inwardly. Stanley Funnell . . . masters were just men after all. He seemed surprised at the thought, and he looked at Mr Funnell as he replied to the farmer, 'It's always changing; it never looks the same twice. But it gets more beautiful each year. I've promised myself to come up in the winter and I will.'

'Do that. Do that,' said Mr Walsh. 'But I bet you one thing. You won't stand like you're doing now, not at this height. In fact, there's been times when I've had to go over the slope on me hands and knees.'

'Indeed I quite believe it.' Mr Funnell nodded his head. Then turning to Matty, he said, 'Well, what do you think about it?'

'It's wonderful, sir.'

'You really think that?'

'Aye. Yes. Yes, I do.'

'Would you get tired of seeing it every day?'

'Me!' Matty answered quickly. 'No, no, I wouldn't get tired of seeing it every day.' His attention was now drawn from Mr Funnell to Mr Walsh, for the farmer was staring hard at him and his expression was very odd. His eyes were half-closed and his face unsmiling, and Matty said once again to himself, 'He doesn't cotton on to me.'

Matty dropped his gaze from the farmer, and, embarrassed now, he walked to where the two boys and Jessica were sitting perched on a shelf of rock. And when he came up to them, Jessica put a question to him. 'Does it scare you being up

140

high like this?' She sounded as if she hoped it did, and he smiled at her, a superior smile, as he said, 'No, I'm not frightened of heights. Are you?' She seemed surprised at the question, and she tilted her chin up at him, saying, 'Me, frightened of heights? Of course I'm not. I've climbed nearly to the top of the hump that's behind our house. It's twice the height of this, and all little paths and crannies. And there's sheer drops. I bet you'd be frightened up there because you're not used to climbing.'

Jessica was addressing herself solely to Matty, and, he thought, in a way designed to belittle him. She was like her father, she had it in for him. Well, let her. It didn't matter. Girls only liked fellows like Willie who could make them laugh, or little fellows like Joe, whom they could patronize.

Jessica said now, 'I bet you wouldn't dare go up the hump.'

'Perhaps I wouldn't.' He raised his eyebrows and turned from her. What was up with her? She seemed set for a row.

He was glad when he saw Mr Walsh and Mr Funnell move off down into the valley, and then for the next half-an-hour he forgot entirely about Jessica, or the boys, as he watched the two dogs, under Mr Walsh's direction, separate six sheep from the herd, then skilfully, and without fluster, bring them down to a walled field near the farm.

The day turned out to be one of the most successful of the holiday, at least in Willie's and Joe's opinion, when Mrs Walsh invited them all over to tea. Nor was there any further talk about going home on the morrow now because Mr Walsh had asked them if they would like a run into Hexham again. He was taking the six sheep to a butcher. These, he had explained to them, were a special order, and if they didn't mind sitting among the trussed-up sheep they were welcome.

Mr Walsh, who seemed in a very amiable mood, naturally included Matty in the invitation, and when, hesitantly, Matty had thanked him, but added that if it was the same to him he would just as soon stay on the farm, Mr Walsh had bestowed upon him again that odd look, which made Matty think why the heck hadn't he kept his mouth shut and just gone with the others?

That night as they got ready for bed there was a lot of talk, as usual mostly between Willie and Joe. But it was when they were tucked up in their sleeping bags that Joe first touched on the controversial subject of slaughtering sheep, and the more personal one of having to ride in the same lorry. 'It's awful, man,' he said to Matty. 'There, the poor things'll be lying all trussed up, and in an hour or so they'll be dead.'

'You'd think,' Willie called from his tent, 'bringing them up and lookin' after them, he just couldn't take them to the slaughter-house. It's sort of heartless, isn't it?'

'Aye,' said Joe. 'And you know, Jessica said they brought a dozen up on the bottle last year; she used to feed them.'

'It's cruel,' said Willie. 'Say what you like, it's cruel.'

'You eat meat, don't you?' Matty was sitting bolt upright now.

'What did you say, Matty?' Willie was pretending he hadn't heard.

'I said, you eat meat.'

'Aye, of course I do,' came Willie's voice.

'And you eat lamb, don't you?' Matty was

142

bellowing down on Joe now, and Joe said, 'Aye. Aye, I suppose I do.'

'Well, you don't object to eating lamb and beef, do you?'

'That's not the point,' shouted Willie.

'It is the point, only you're too thick-headed to see it.' Matty was snapping now. 'That's what you breed the sheep and the cattle for; they're not pets. You eat bacon, don't you, and chicken? You don't go goofy about a chicken. Your dad keeps chickens, doesn't he? Do you cry your eyes out when he kills one?'

There was a short silence following this last remark. Then Willie's tone, stiff now, saying, 'I thought you were fond of animals? You're the one that's supposed to go crackers about dogs.'

'Dogs are different. You have a dog as a friend, same as a cat, or a bird. Not that I hold with birds in cages. But animals on farms are different; they are reared for meat; they are reared to be eaten.'

'I can't understand you. Honest, I can't.'

'Well, don't strain yourself,' Matty called back. Then turning towards Joe and speaking more quietly, he asked, 'You see the point?'

Joe wriggled in his bag; then said, 'No. No, Matty. Honest I don't. I can't see how you can go crackers over a dog and then don't get worked up over those poor sheep going to the slaughter-house the morrow.'

'Well then,' said Matty, 'I'll tell you what. I'll make a bargain with you. I'll get worked up over sheep going to the slaughter-house if you promise not to eat any beef, or lamb, or bacon or chicken ever again. How about it?'

'Aw, don't be daft, man. It's as Willie says, you're funny.'

'Oh, he does, does he?'

'Aw, he didn't mean that . . . he just meant . . .'

'I know what he meant. So I'm funny. Well I'm going to remain funny. Good-night. And if you can't go to sleep try counting the sheep going into the slaughter-house.'

Joe started to laugh, a low rumbling, choking sound, and it was so infectious that Matty found himself having to keep his hand hard across his mouth not to join in. Then when Willie's high yelp came from the other tent he let his laughter burst from him.

So the argument ended in laughter, and soon they were all asleep.

9

The clouds, low on the hill, gave warning of a storm to come as Mr Walsh put the last wriggling sheep into the back of the lorry and heaved Willie and Joe up, to act as their nursemaids – Mr Walsh's own term for them. Lastly, he ordered Prince up. Then looking towards the sky, he said, 'I reckon we've missed that lot; it's rolling hard towards the coast'; adding quickly, 'Let's get going.' He kissed his wife and Jessica. But before he mounted the cab he turned slowly and looked at Matty, where he was standing next to Mr Funnell. He looked at him with that deep penetrating stare of his, and said with a half smile, 'Well, it's all yours. I'm leaving you in charge.'

Matty cast a swift glance at Mr Funnell thinking that remark must apply to him; then, digging his thumb in his chest, he said, 'You mean me?'

'Yes, of course, I mean you. You said you wanted to stay behind and work, didn't you?'

'Yes. Yes, I did.'

'Well then, get on with it. And you'll be answerable to me when I get back if anything goes wrong.' He was laughing now. It was a joke, and Matty laughed too. And Willie and Joe laughed, their voices rising above the bleating of the sheep. And Mrs Walsh laughed, and Jessica laughed . . . but Mr Funnell didn't laugh. As the engine started and he reached one hand toward the door of the cab to take his seat beside the farmer, he turned to Matty and said quickly, 'Act as if that was an order. Understand?'

Matty blinked, then nodded. But he wasn't quite sure in his own mind what he had to understand at this particular point. Then Mr Funnell added, 'Remember what I told you earlier on. Remember?'

Again Matty nodded.

'Good-bye then, and the best of luck, Matty.'

'Good-bye, sir, and the same to you.' Matty was smiling warmly at the master. It was the first time Mr Funnell had called him by his Christian name, and as the lorry rolled away down the hill and Mrs Walsh and Jessica leant against each other and laughed at the antics of Willie and Joe as they held their noses and stared at the sheep in mock disgust, Matty was remembering what Mr Funnell had said. 'Talk,' he had said. 'Open out to Mr Walsh. Let him see what you are made of. Don't give him the impression that you're surly. And remember, if you want anything in this life you've got to go after it, and you've got to show you care about it. Do you understand?'

He had understood that all right, but he couldn't say to Mr Funnell that he didn't think that he'd ever be able to show Mr Walsh he cared, not about the particular subject they were both discussing, the unnamed subject. They might have gone into it more fully if they'd had any time alone, but there'd been Willie and Joe milling about all the time, or Jessica. Still he'd known what the master was hinting at all right. And now he was asking himself why Mr Walsh

146

had said, 'I'm leaving you in charge.' Probably the farmer was pulling his leg. Even if Mr Funnell had put him in the picture and said, 'Matty Doolin has a way with animals,' Mr Walsh would never pick on him, for the simple reason that he didn't cotton on to him. Now if it had been Willie, or even Joe, something might have come of it, but not him. And all because he couldn't make his tongue wag. 'Tell him. *Talk!*' Mr Funnell had said. It was all right for people to say that who could talk themselves, whose tongues could 'clip clouts' as the saying went. Not that Mr Funnell was a great talker; but still he was never lost for words. At this moment it appeared to Matty that he was the only one in the world who was lost for words, the right words.

'I bet they'll be glad when they get to Hexham; what do you think?'

'Oh, aye, Mrs Walsh. I bet they will.' Matty dragged his attention to her.

'They'll be mixed up with the sheep before they're at the bottom of the hill . . . poor sheep.' As Jessica finished speaking she turned to Matty and added, 'If you had gone there'd have been less room still. You'd have had to nurse one on your knees. You wouldn't have liked that.'

'Go on with you.' Her mother pushed her. Then turning to Matty, she said, 'Well now, where are we going to start first?'

'Wherever you like, Mrs Walsh,' he said, patting Betsy as he spoke.

'No, it's wherever you like. Take your choice. There's the byres to be sluiced, feed to carry, and there's the pig sties to be cleaned. I think that's enough to be going on with. For me I'm going to see to my chickens, and then I'm going to get up some butter. After that, there's the dinner to see

147

to, and then I've got some baking to do. That'll carry me on to the milking, so my day's planned.'

'I'll start on the cow byres first.'

'Whatever you like ... Your mother won't recognize those shorts when you get home.'

'Aw, it won't matter. I don't suppose I'll be wearing them again; you can't go around the docks in shorts.'

She gave him a long intense look, very like her husband's, then said, 'No, you're right there. You can't go around the docks in shorts, yet' – she laughed now – 'when I was young I used to see the coolies coming out of the gates at Tyne Dock and going up the Station Bank, one after the other, wearing only a singlet and short pants, so I suppose you could go into the docks in shorts?' Matty laughed with her now.

When they reached the farmyard he gave her a nod and, saying no more, went into the cow shed.

The swilling of the cow sheds would have been a very pleasurable occupation if it hadn't been for Jessica. The carrying of the grain and the hay from the main barn to the storeroom would have been equally pleasant, if it hadn't been for Jessica. The cleaning of the pig sties, not a pleasant job at any time, but one that he didn't really mind, would have been got through in half the time if it hadn't been for Jessica ... and her questions. Where did he live? What was it like? How old was his mother? What was his father called besides Doolin? Were they old? What was his best subject at school? This was a difficult one. Did he like Mr Funnell? Mr Funnell was all right, he said. Did he know that Mr Funnell liked him? He gave no answer to this. Did he know that her mother liked him? All he could say to this was, 'Oh?' How much money would he get when

148

he started working in the docks? Perhaps six or seven pounds a week to start with. This seemed to shatter her. Why that was nearly twice as much as any boy would get who started on a farm. What would he do with all that money?

He had answered her questions without looking at her, until she asked, 'Have you got a girl?'

'A girl!' He turned his head disdainfully. 'No, I haven't got a girl. What do I want with a girl?'

'Willie has,' she said.

'Willie would have,' he replied, 'if he got the chance, but he's kidding you.'

'He wasn't kidding me. Why are you always grumpy?'

'I'm not always grumpy.'

'You have been since you've been here.'

He stared at her for a moment, then said brusquely, 'Get out of my road, or you'll get splashed.'

Jessica moved out of his way, then stood surveying him for some time before saying, in a very small voice, 'You never say anything nice to anybody, do you?'

Matty slowly straightened himself and stared at her as she walked away. He wanted to call her back but he knew he hadn't the words; it was no good.

It was around three o'clock when Matty, who was working in the big barn trying to bring some order into the jumble of old machine parts, realized that at least this time Mr Walsh was wrong with regard to the weather, for the storm hadn't blown itself to the coast but was bursting in the hills inland. Although a good distance away, the roll of the thunder came to him every now and again, and he thought that if it looked like being a wet night he'd ask Mr Walsh if they could kip in the barn.

'Matty! Matty!' As he heard his name called he ran from the barn into the yard and saw Mrs Walsh standing outside the kitchen door, and as she waved to him he went towards her, still running. There was a man with her and she said quickly, 'This is my brother, Mr Reid, Matty. He's come to take me down to Slaggyford; our other brother is very ill. Have you seen Jessica?'

'No, Mrs Walsh. Not since dinner-time.'

'She'll be gone up the hump. She had her airs about something at dinner-time. I could see that. Likely because her father didn't take her into Hexham. When she gets in a huff she always goes up there. Look, Matty, if she's not back within fifteen minutes send Betsy for her. Just say to her, "Fetch . . . Fetch, Jessica." Go to the far gate, the one that's in the wall running round the bottom of the hill. You know, over there.' She pointed. 'And just say that to her and point towards the fells, and she'll find her.'

'Yes, I'll do that, Mrs Walsh.'

'I don't suppose I'll be back before my husband now, but he'll be in time for the milking. It can't be helped if it's a little late. The cows may kick up a row, but take no notice. He won't be all that late. I'll leave a note for him anyway . . . Tell Jessica that she's got to make your teas. I'm sorry I've got to go off like this, Matty.'

'Oh, it's all right, Mrs Walsh, I'll see to things; at least the things I can do. If Mr Walsh isn't back when it's time, shall I bring the cows in?'

'Yes, you could do that, Matty. That would be a help.'

He nodded brightly at her.

'I'll get my things.' Mrs Walsh nodded at her

brother before going into the house, and he, looking at Matty said, 'You one of the boys camping here?'

'Yes,' said Matty.

'Like it?'

'Oh, yes. Very much.'

'Yes, you will for a time. But you'd soon get tired of it. Farming isn't everybody's game. It's all right now, but in the winter . . . Eeh! By gum, I've seen my brother-in-law with icicles hanging off his nose, and I'm not funnin'.'

Mrs Walsh now came out of the house, pulling on her coat, and she looked up to the sky, saying, 'Oh dear me, I do hope it doesn't come this way. Look, Matty, I tell you what you'd better do. Go up to the foot of the hill there now and call her. Shout her name . . . like this.' She cupped her hands over her mouth, making a funnel. 'And send the dog off at the same time. You'll do that?'

'Yes, Mrs Walsh, straight away. I'll go now. Come on, Betsy.' The dog who was lying on the mat to the side of the kitchen door sprang up immediately and followed him.

When he reached the far wall, Matty could just see the outline of the foothills, and, bending down to the dog, he said slowly, 'Fetch. Fetch Jessica, Betsy.' Immediately Betsy answered the command and bounded towards the hills. The next minute she was lost in a swirling mass of mist.

Putting his hands to his mouth he called, 'Jes-si-ca. Oo! Oo! Jes-si-ca.'

Now the mist was rolling swiftly towards him, and with it came an icy wind. The atmosphere had suddenly become so cold that he shivered and hugged himself with his crossed arms. Again he called, 'Jes-si-ca! Jes-si-ca!' And yet again. But now his voice seemed to come back at him as if it was rebounding softly off the wall of mist. Within minutes the mist had enveloped him and the whole of the farm, and when he turned round he could just make out the dim shapes of the buildings.

When he shouted now it was like speaking into a blanket. He wished, oh, how he wished Mrs Walsh hadn't gone away. If only there was someone on the farm.

He knew he'd have to get a coat; he was shivering. He went now, at a groping trot, towards the farm, through the yard and down the road to the field, and when he passed through the gate it was as if he had walked into another world, for here, strangely, there was no mist. It was dull, and cold, but quite clear. Hurrying now, he made for the tent, grabbed up a thick pullover and pulled it on over his thin shirt, and, taking up his mack, put that on too, then pelted back to the farm.

He came to an abrupt stop in the middle of the yard, and watched, fascinated, the mist rolling back like a curtain over the roof of the farmhouse. Thank goodness. It was just a temporary thing. The mist scared him more than the storm, far more. It had an eerie sort of feeling, the mist. He ran on to the far wall and, again looking towards the hills, he began to call. He called until his throat was sore, and he watched the mist covering and uncovering the hills as if someone was playing a game with giant curtains.

Half-an-hour later, Matty stood in the farm kitchen looking at the clock, and he was frightened. The dog had not returned, nor had Jessica. That dog could go miles within half-an-hour. If only somebody would come; he didn't mind who, if only somebody. At that moment he felt the

152

whole weight of the farm on his shoulders, but even more he felt the responsibility for Jessica.

He knew that if the dog had found Jessica and she was all right, the dog would have brought her back ... If the dog had found Jessica and she wasn't all right, then the dog would have come back on her own for help. So, if the dog *hadn't* come back, *both* of them were in trouble.

He set off for the hump.

As he drew nearer to it he made out, from the parts he could see, that it was a very large hill, or as Mr Walsh would have said, a young mountain. The nearer he approached to it the steeper it appeared; and its sides looked dark green, smooth and shiny.

Before he started the ascent up the narrow winding path he put his hands to his mouth and called again; then listened. Again he called, and again he listened, but no sound came to him. Now, added to the odd feeling that was drawing him on, was an eeriness that was almost tangible. He felt alone in a terrifying way, as if there never had been, nor ever would be, anyone in this place but himself.

He did not know how long he had been climbing but he could see that he had reached a good height. For want of breath he stopped, and when he tried, once again, to call, he made very little sound. The top of the hump seemed only a short distance away and he now quickened his scrambling to reach it. It looked flat from where he had last viewed it.

Finally, when with an effort he pulled himself up an almost vertical rock onto what he thought was the top of this young mountain, he stood gasping.

In every direction he looked, except backward,

the land seemed to rise higher, and yet higher.
He had half expected to look down into some
kind of valley similar to that which he had
seen when he had gone over the mountain with
Mr Walsh on the other side of the farm. He
couldn't imagine how all this terrifying rough
cragland managed to hide behind the hump. He
viewed the comparatively small hill now as a kind
of ordinary dream leading into a nightmare.
Where would he start looking from here?

'Jessica! Jessica!' He was calling again loudly,
his fear giving strength to his voice. He began to
move forward slowly. He mustn't get lost up
here, and he must get back down to the farm the
way he came. If he lost his way that would make
three of them.

'Jessica! Jessica! Oo! Oo! Jessica.'

It was as if the giant that controlled the curtains had heard his call and become angry at the
disturbance, for as quickly as if created by a
magician's wand there came rolling towards him
a great bank of mist, and he stood stiff, almost
petrified, as it enfolded him. This was different
mist from that which had enveloped him and the
farm earlier; it was heavy, and clinging, and cold,
and it brought him hunched down on to the rock.

Eeh! He'd have to get out of this, he'd have to.
He couldn't just sit there, he'd go crackers. He
knew which way he had come; it wasn't very far
to the path that led down the hump. Once on that,
he would be all right. He turned in what he imagined was the right direction, and, making things
doubly safe, went on his hands and knees.

A few minutes later he stopped. His whole
body was trembling, his knees, his teeth, even his
hands. He had missed it. It wasn't this far away;
he was sure it wasn't. Now fear urged him on

until quite suddenly he felt the ground slope away, and under his hands and knees was the path. He knew it was the path; he could feel it was the path. Going backwards now he crawled slowly and carefully along its winding trail. Down and down he went, his heart much lighter now. He should be near the bottom. It didn't seem half as steep going down as it did coming up.

The mist, playing its pranks again, lifted and revealed in one frightening moment why the path didn't appear so steep; he just wasn't on a path at all!

Quickly he rose to his feet and the mist as quickly rolled away from him as if to show him his new surroundings. He was on the side of a rock and all round rose other rocks. He bit on his lip to stop its trembling; and his legs became so weak he went to sit down but checked himself. He must keep moving; as long as he could see where he was going, he must keep moving.

And he kept moving, but with each step the panic seemed to rise in him. He rounded a bend in the rocks and came to a dead stop, for there only a few feet away the rock dropped almost vertically.

With his back pressed tight against the wall of rock he put his hand up and wiped his face. The moisture on it was not only from the mist but from the sweat of fear that was oozing from him.

More to comfort himself with the sound of his voice than for any other reason, he put his hands to his trembling lips and called Jessica's name again. And this time he received an answer. It came in an echo from the rocks that formed an amphitheatre below him. It was a dim, far-away echo, and had that eerie sound. Then he gulped in his throat and checked his breathing to listen to another sound on the tail of the echo, a sound that was not a reproduction of any he had made. It came as a whimper; then as a faint bark; then a whimper again.

Betsy! Betsy was somewhere near. He almost jumped forward in his excitement, only in time did he remember the big drop in front of him.

Hands to mouth again, he called, 'Jessica! Jessica!' And when the echo died away, there it was again: two barks this time and no whimper, and it came from straight on ahead, not down below in the swirling mist, or behind him, but straight on.

He could see only a few yards ahead now, and, cautiously feeling his way with both feet and hands, he moved along the rock wall, stopping at intervals to call, and hearing clearer and clearer Betsy's answering bark.

He was shivering now with relief when from just beyond the curtain of mist Betsy barked again.

He never knew what it was that forced him to his knees and prompted caution at this point. Whether it was some message he picked up from the tone of the dog's bark, or a natural protective instinct, but he had crawled no more than a couple of yards when he saw he was on the edge of another drop. Yet it was from seeming space that Betsy's whine now came to him.

Lying flat on his stomach he wriggled forward, and when he put his head over the edge of the cliff he could have laughed with relief if the circumstances hadn't been so terrifying, and the plight of Betsy so pitiful, for there, not a foot below him, she lay, her eyes looking up into his.

He remained perfectly still staring down at the dog, and she remained still while looking up at him, for she was fully aware that one false move and she would topple from the narrow ledge on which she lay into the void below.

Quickly Matty's eyes passed over her. He had been puzzled at first why she hadn't jumped the short distance from the ledge on to the rock again. And then he saw the reason for her stillness. Betsy was lying on the narrowest edge of the ledge. To the right of her it widened out to a distance of about four feet, but the whole ledge, he saw immediately, was pitted with small crevices and loose boulders. These were the reasons for Betsy's stillness, for one of her back paws was in a small crevice, and pinning it there was the edge of a boulder. Matty saw that her leg was torn and bleeding where she had bitten at it, trying to free it.

'Quiet! Quiet!' His own voice demonstrated the word, and as he put his hands down to her he repeated, 'Quiet, Betsy. Quiet.'

One hand firmly on her neck, he held her still while he eased up the boulder from her leg, and when he pushed it backwards it rolled and went hurtling over the edge into the mist, and the sound of it bouncing from rock to rock brought a sickness to his stomach.

His voice now firmer still, he warned her, 'Quiet! Quiet!' Then simultaneously gripping her collar and the back of her haunches, he levered her on to her three feet; then with a final pull she was beside him.

'Aw, Betsy. Betsy. You're all right. You're all right.' He was almost crying with his relief, and the dog, after licking his face twice, dropped slowly down by his side and, turning her head to her damaged paw, began to lick that.

Matty now wiped the mist and sweat from his

eyes and looked more closely at the dog's foot.
And as he did so he groaned for besides the rent
in the flesh it was plain, even to his inexperienced
eye, that the ankle bone was broken.

'Aw, Betsy, Betsy.' He fondled her head. 'Now
we're in a worse state than ever.' He pressed her
close to his side and she seemed content to lie
there for a few minutes. Then painfully she struggled to her feet and, after limping on her three
paws, she stopped and turned her head towards
him, the look in her eyes saying plainly, 'Come
on.' And obediently he followed her.

The dog's progress was excruciatingly slow
and painful, and every step hurt Matty. That the
dog obviously knew where she was going was
evident, because, the mist clearing again, he saw
before him the clear imprint of two paths, one
branching off to the right round the side of the
mountain, the other going steeply downwards. It
was this latter path that Betsy took, and caused
Matty to protest, 'Stay, girl. Stay.' Betsy
stopped, but only long enough to look up at him
before moving painfully and cautiously on again.

The mist was being aided now by a wind, a wet
wind, that bore on it a drizzle that was even
colder than the mist itself, and Matty shivered as
he stood watching Betsy sniffing at a point on a
grassy slope to the side of the rough path where
flowers were growing in the rocks. Dropping on
to his hunkers, he said, 'Where is she? Where's
Jessica? Find Jessica.' At this, Betsy sniffed
wildly about her. It was evident Jessica had been
here. This was where the dog thought he would
find her, among these flowers.

It was with little hope of an answer that Matty
once again put his hands to his mouth and called,
'Jessica! Jessica! Oo! Oo! Jessica!' And when

now faintly there came back to him a reply of 'Oo! Oo!' he patted the dog's head excitedly and cried, 'That's her. That's her, Betsy. Find her!'

Obediently, Betsy went on, but her walk was even slower for she was obviously in great pain. At intervals Matty would stop and call, and each time Jessica's answer came nearer. And then he saw her. Through the drizzling rain he caught a glimpse of her figure. She seemed to be standing in the air above his head. The next minute she came slithering and calling down the rocks towards him.

'Oh, Matty. Matty.' She grabbed at his arm with one hand while patting the dog with the other. Then, her wild movements stopping abruptly, she cried, 'What's the matter with her? What happened to her foot?'

'Don't touch it.' Matty looked down on her where she was kneeling by the dog. 'She's broken her paw.'

'Oh, no. No. Oh, Betsy, I'm sorry. I am, I am.'

'Well, it wasn't your fault.' He drew his hand over the top of his head, pressing the water off his hair. He was actually smiling, so great was his relief. The fact that they had to get home didn't bother him at this point – he had found her, and the dog.

'I'm sorry, Matty.' She was standing gazing up at him, as she apologized. And he said airily, 'There's nothing to be sorry about. You couldn't help it; anybody would get lost in this.'

'I could help it, I could.' As she pushed the wet hair out of her eyes he said briskly, 'Well, we won't go into that now; we'll have to get back. Do you know the road?'

She peered up at him, then said slowly and flatly, 'If I knew the road, I wouldn't be here, would I?'

He felt as if he had received a slap, and he told

159

himself she was quite right; if she knew the road she wouldn't be here. 'But I thought you knew every inch of the hump,' he said quietly.

'But this isn't the hump; we're miles off the hump.'

'Miles!' His lips left his teeth bare.

'Yes, and it's my fault.' Her voice was trembling and he said again, 'Well, we won't go into it now. We'd better follow Betsy, and she'll take us home.'

They both turned their attention to the dog now and were equally surprised to see that she had moved a few yards from them and was lying down under the shelter of an overhanging jut of rock.

'She's bad.' Jessica was kneeling beside her again. 'She wouldn't be like this unless she was really bad.'

Betsy lay still, her head on the ground, only her eyes moving as she looked up at them.

'She can't go on, that's plain.' Matty, also kneeling beside the dog, lifted her head on to his knee. Then he looked at Jessica and asked, 'Have you no idea of the way back?'

'Not unless it clears up. If I got on a high enough rock and could see the hump . . . Oh, I'm sorry.' She dropped her chin on to her breast. 'It's my fault. It's all my fault we're in this mess.'

'Don't keep on sayin' that. You got lost and that's that.'

'I wasn't lost, not at first, not when you first started to call.'

He raised his eyes from the dog, and his voice was gruff as he asked her, 'You heard me call?'

He watched her nod her head. 'You mean to say you heard me call and you wouldn't come, or answer? Why?'

160

It was some seconds before she said, 'I wanted you to come up the hump, and then I was going to jump out on you and give you a fright.'

'Oh.' He sounded as if he understood, but he didn't, not until she added, 'You wouldn't talk and . . . and it gets so lonely in the holidays.' Her head sunk lower, and Matty hardly knew where to look when he heard her crying.

'Aw now, now. Give over. Come on, there's nothing to cry about.' His finger tentatively touched her shoulder. 'I'm always grumpy, that's me.' He gave a shaky laugh. 'The lads told you, didn't they? That's me, I don't mean anything.' He became aware as he talked that her dress was wet and he exclaimed quickly, 'Why, you're soaked to the skin. I didn't realize you'd got no coat on . . . Here.'

As he pulled off his mack she protested, 'No, no. You keep dry; I'm wet already, it doesn't matter.'

'Do what you're told for once.' He thrust the coat roughly around her, then said, 'Look. Let's do what Betsy's doing, keep close to the rock. We'll escape a little wet that way. Come on.' He pulled her towards the dog, and they sat, one on each side of her, with their backs to the rock, and as they stared into the driving rain a silence fell upon them, until Matty said, in a small voice, 'How long do these storms last?'

'You never can tell.'

'No?'

'If it doesn't clear before dark, it could go on all night.' Her voice was so low he barely caught her words, and he didn't repeat, 'All night?' but the words galloped through his mind and brought the fear galloping back into his body. All night! Up here like this. He was wet to the skin now, and cold, and it wasn't as cold as it would be in the night ... But they wouldn't be here all night. Folk would come searching for them, Mr Walsh and the other farmers. Yet would they, unless Mrs Walsh came back?

As he heard a shuddering sob coming from Jessica, he forgot his own fear for a moment, and said, 'Now, now. It'll be all right. You'll see. This can't keep up for very long anyway, it's too heavy, and then we'll make our way down, careful like.'

'Father will be mad at me. He's always told me not to go beyond ... beyond the shelf.'

'Where's that?'

'It's the level piece on top of the hump.'

'Well.' He tried to make his voice light. 'Why didn't you wait for me *there* to give me a fright?'

'I ... I don't know.' She was stammering now. 'I ... I just thought, I would run a little way over the fells, and get on some higher place and watch you when you reached the top of the hump. I thought when you didn't keep calling you were up here coming. And then the mist came down – it had been clear up here – and when I tried to find the path again I couldn't. And then I realized I wasn't where I thought I was and I got frightened and began to scramble about. I knew I was lost and when the mist cleared I kept running and running. I ... I've never been this way. Father says it's the worst part of the fells; it's like a maze. They call it The Bowl; The Devil's Bowl. Oh, he'll be mad at me and Mother'll be so worried.'

'Now, now. You won't make it any better cryin', will you?' He felt her shivering and asked, 'Are you still cold?'

'Y-e-s, but not so bad. You must be frozen. I

feel awful having your coat. Look; take half of it. We'll put it in front of us.'

'You leave it alone.' Reaching out, he stopped her hand unbuttoning the coat. 'Curl your legs underneath you. Better still, I'll change places and sit yon side of you, and you move up gently into Betsy's back. She'll like that. It'll sort of comfort her, and you'll keep each other warm.'

He stood up, and she edged along closer towards the dog.

Once settled, they sat silently as the rain beat against their faces.

'What time do you think it is?'

He thought for a minute. 'Around six, I should say.'

'Tea-time.' Her voice was very, very small. 'Mother was going to give you a slap-up tea.'

'Well' – he endeavoured to make his answer light – 'she will yet. Coo! let me get at it. I'll start off with six cups, then gollop ten slices of bread and butter, jam and cream, six pieces of lardy cake, and finish up with half-a-dozen scones, a sponge cake, and a jam roll.'

She didn't laugh but said, 'Father'll blame me for breaking Betsy's paw. He's very fond of Betsy, she's his favourite. He says she's the wisest dog he's ever had.'

'Now, now look.' He turned towards her. 'He'll be so glad to see you he won't even raise his voice.'

To this piece of comfort Jessica sniffed and said, enigmatically, 'You won't ever want to work on a farm now, will you?'

'How did you know I wanted to work on a farm?'

He watched her shake her head as she went on, 'But you won't now because you'd have to go out

163

nights like this to see to the cattle, only it would be much colder. So you wouldn't want to do that, would you?'

'If I'd just had those six cups of tea, and ten slices of bread and jam, etc. etc., I don't think I'd mind.'

'You wouldn't?'

'No.'

'Oh.'

As the silence fell on them once more he thought: She's a funny kid really. Nice but funny. But how did she know he wanted to work on a farm? Unless Willie and Joe had been yapping to her. Yet he had never told them that he had wanted to work on a farm. He had never told anybody except Mr Funnell . . . Mr Funnell?

'Matty, they're not going to come. Should we try to find a way down?' Her voice had a high cracking sound to it, and he answered sharply, 'No! No! That would be daft. I don't know me way, and you don't know the way. The only one who could get us back is Betsy, and she is past it. Look at her.' He bent in front of Jessica and looked at the dog. Betsy was breathing deeply but lying quite still. Her body, although wringing wet, was giving off a great deal of heat and she was evidently in great pain.

If the dog had been on its own, Matty thought, it would have made its way back to the farm somehow, but having found its mistress, it was waiting for its master to come and find them. And who was he, a townite, to pit his wits against the sure knowledge of a hill dog? Yet he had to reassure Jessica, for she was getting, what his mother called, all worked up.

'I tell you what we could do,' he said eagerly. 'We could keep calling. There might be somebody else up here, somebody who knows the way.'

'Yes, there might. That's a good idea. We'll take turns, eh? You go first.'

Cupping his hands over his mouth, Matty now called, 'Hello there! Hello! Hello!' He did this a number of times. Then Jessica took on the call. 'Hello! Hello! Hello!' With each call they made, the dog moved uneasily. Once she got to her feet, only to collapse slowly again on her side. But as they called she kept raising her head as if she was listening.

After fifteen minutes their throats were sore, and Matty said, 'Let's give it a rest for a time.' And to this Jessica replied dolefully, 'I don't suppose it'll do any good anyway, the wind's too strong and it's getting worse. It's ... it'll be a gale ... Eeh! Eeh! I don't know what Father will say to me.' As her head drooped on to her chest, Matty shyly put his hand onto her shoulder again, saying, "There, now. I tell you he'll be so pleased to see you he'll throw a party.' When she turned and buried her face in his neck he blinked rapidly with embarrassment, but gallantly went on patting her.

It was almost dark when Matty, pulling his pullover from over his head, said gruffly, 'Here, stick your legs through the arms and pull it over your dress, up under your coat.'

'No, no. You've got nothing on, only your shirt.'

'I couldn't be any wetter, so it doesn't matter.'

'You'll be frozen. You ... you are frozen.'

Strangely, Matty didn't feel so cold now; his body felt numb, as if he had been beaten all over with small sharp-pointed sticks. He wasn't any longer even very much aware of the rain. He only knew that he felt uneasy about the way Jessica was shivering and that he'd have to do something about it.

He was getting a little confused now. He kept hearing Mr Walsh's voice saying, 'You're in charge. You're in charge,' and he couldn't understand why no one had come in search of them. It was now almost dark and must be nearing ten o'clock. Folk were bound to have realized that they were missing before now. He just couldn't reason it out.

But there was this business of keeping Jessica warm; at least, not warm but less cold; so he gave her his pullover under the assumption that the weight of the wet clothes might help. And now he had another hazy idea, and he thought he'd better put it into action before he fell asleep because he was feeling very drowsy. He couldn't understand why he should feel so drowsy.

'Look,' he said slowly. 'They're bound to be here shortly. Now lie down on your side with your back to Betsy's back. I'll move her so her paw is near the wall . . . there, like that. You'll soon feel the heat of her coming right through you. And I'll lie in front of you.' He lay down in front of her now and asked, 'Is that better?'

'Ye . . . yes.'

'Well, you won't feel much different for a few minutes, but you'll get warm, you'll see.'

He lay with his head on his arm and he no longer felt the cold of the stone beneath him. He knew that he should be on his feet yelling into the night, but he couldn't yell any more; he was too tired, he was all in. As he went to sleep he wondered if he would ever see his mother again. This was what she had feared, him getting lost on the hills. It was funny about that. Yes, it was very

funny when he came to think about it. That had
been her great fear, that if he went camping or
tramping he'd get lost and die on some mountain.
It was funny ... funny the way things turned
out. She must have had one of those premonitions, sort of.

10

It was two o'clock in the morning before the search party found them. A section of it, headed by Mr Funnell, was guided to them by Betsy's whining.

Matty couldn't remember anything of the descent, but he had a vague memory of having been woken up during some period in the far, far past, with people fussing him, and he wishing they wouldn't. He had just wanted to be let alone, for he felt very tired.

He still felt very tired. He had been lying for some time now with his eyes closed listening to the murmur of voices. He didn't ask himself where he was, but he thought he was dreaming a bit, for at one point he imagined he heard the mooing of the cows, and straight after this he was sure he heard his mother's voice whispering. That proved conclusively to him that he was dreaming.

His eyelids flickered, then closed again. It was daylight, bright, sunshining daylight.

'Matty, are you awake?'

He made an effort and pushed his heavy eyelids upwards; there to see Mrs Walsh's face above him.

'Would you like something to drink?' Her voice was soft.

Mrs Walsh was asking him if he would like

something to drink. He couldn't get himself sorted out but he felt thirsty, very thirsty, and he was hot and sweating. But he shouldn't be hot, should he? He should be cold and wet. He stretched his eyes to keep them open and said, 'Jessica?'

'She's all right. She's all right.' Mrs Walsh's voice was trembling, and to his amazement she bent down and kissed him. Three times she kissed him. Now Mrs Walsh was smiling at him. Her face was all wet with tears but she was smiling, and her voice had a cracked sound as she said, 'Don't you want to see who's here?' She looked to the side of him, and when he turned his head and saw his mother sitting at the bedside he thought again, I must be dreaming, but when she took his hand and held it tightly, he said quickly, 'Hello, Mam.'

'Hello, son.'

'How did you get here?'

'Oh, that's a long story.'

When he heard the door click and he knew Mrs Walsh had left the room, he attempted to pull himself up on to his elbow, but his mother checked him, and, patting the clothes under his chin, she said, 'Now lie quiet; you're very hot.'

'But, Mam.'

'Don't talk; just lie still. If you'll lie still I'll go and call your dad.'

'Me dad!' Again he got up on his elbow, only to be pressed back. 'But what's he doing here? Me dad.'

'It was him that heard on the late news about it all and nothing would stop him. He phoned the police at Hexham, and got the last train up to Newcastle, and a lift on a lorry to Hexham from there. And your dad went to hire a car, but there was a reporter in the garage and he brought us the rest of the way. They had got you all down when we arrived . . . Oh, Matty.' She was bending over him now, his hand pressed against her chest.

Matty looked up at his mother sadly. He knew her worst fears had come true. If ever she needed a seal to put on his sentence in the docks she had it now.

Perhaps it was the look on his face that made her speak what was near her heart at this moment, for she said softly and hesitantly, 'I said to your dad, if . . . if they find him and he's all right he can do what he likes in the future. As long as he's all right, that's all that matters.'

'Mam!'

'That's what I said. And your dad said with me, "Aye . . . aye, life's short, but short, or long, it's his own and he should do what he wants with it . . ." And you know, I . . . I thought it was very strange when Mr Walsh told us about him going to offer you the job.'

'The . . . the job?'

'Yes.' She nodded slowly at him. 'Before you came home he was going to put it to you. He'd been thinking for a long time he needed help, and' – she touched his hot cheek – 'he's taken with you. He said, afore this happened he was taken with you. He said you've not got a lot to say for yourself like the other two, but when you do open your mouth you say something.' She nodded proudly at him.

Matty stared up at his mother, his mouth slightly agape, his eyes wide. He had the impulse to fling his arms about her, and he might have done just that if the door hadn't opened at that moment and Mr Walsh and his father come into the room.

'Well! Well! Well!' This was from Mr Walsh, but he stood aside and let Mr Doolin approach the bed.

Matty, looking up at his father, felt hotter still, if that was possible.

'Hello, lad.'

'Hello, Dad.'

'Feeling all right?'

'Yes, Dad.'

'Well! You've had some excitement, haven't you? Mind you, it won't do you any harm; that's the kind of thing that puts mettle into you in the long run.' He patted his son's head; then turned away, evidently as embarrassed as Matty was with the conversation.

And now Mr Walsh was standing looking down at Matty. 'You did it, then?'

'Did it?'

'The dog would have died if it had been left on that exposed ledge; it was one of the bitterest nights of the year, bar January and February, a freak night. And Jessica would never have found her way out of The Bowl alone, not in that mist. There have been men died there. You were in charge and you carried it out. Jessica's told us all she remembers, and that's enough for the time being. Now . . .' he dug his finger towards Matty. 'You do what the women tell you, right to the letter, for I want you good and well before I let you loose on the farm. Understand?'

Matty slowly moved his head.

'It won't be from eight to five, mind. Sixteen-hour day sometimes, and no double pay for overtime. At least not yet awhile, until you know your business. That understood too?'

Again Matty moved his head.

'Well, I've talked it over here with your father, and your mother.' He nodded towards Mrs Doolin. 'They're agreeable. On one condition.' He smiled towards Mrs Doolin now. 'That you put in an appearance at home once a fortnight. You'll be on every other week-end. Well now, that's enough for the time being. Get yourself to sleep again and sweat it out.'

And now Matty's father was bending over him, his face slightly unfamiliar in its softness.

'Pleased, lad?'

'Oh, aye, Dad. Yes. And thanks.'

Mr Doolin straightened up and, looking at his wife, said,

'Well now. We'll go downstairs and have a bite to eat. Mrs Walsh has had it ready this hour or more. Come on now, come on.' He held out his hand towards his wife, and Mrs Doolin, rising to her feet and leaning over Matty, whispered, 'Go to sleep. That's it; go to sleep. You'll soon be all right.'

Matty fell asleep utterly content. For how long, he didn't know, but when next he awoke he saw by the light that it was late afternoon, and immediately he realized he wasn't alone. He turned his head to the side of the bed, and there, sitting grinning at him, sat Willie and Joe.

'Hello, Matty.'

'Hello, Matty.'

He looked at the two boys for a long moment, then said thickly, 'Hello.'

'How you feelin'?' Joe's voice was very low, as if he was afraid of the sound of it.

'All right.' Matty pushed the clothes away from his chin. 'Bit hot like.'

'You're lucky; you could have died.'

Matty slanted his eyes towards Willie, and he managed to grin as he said, 'Thanks.'

'But he's right, Matty.' Joe's voice was slightly louder now. 'You could have. It said so in the papers.'

172

'In the papers!' Matty screwed his face up at them. 'It's in the papers?'

'Yes, headlines. You're a hero, man.'

'Don't be daft.' Matty sounded his old self now, and Joe said, 'I'm not, man. It said you were practically naked.'

'I wasn't.' Matty's protest was indignant, and strong.

'Well, you know what I mean. It said all about Jessica having your pullover on, the sleeves for legs like, and your coat an' all, and how she was lying atween you and the dog.'

Betsy! For the first time Matty remembered Betsy and, lifting himself upwards, he asked quickly, 'Betsy. How is she?'

'Oh, she's fine. The vet has fixed her foot. The bone was splintered in three places; she must have gone through it.'

'She did.' Matty lay back again.

'You're going to stay on the farm?'

Matty turned and looked at Willie and nodded, saying simply, 'Yes.'

'After last night you still want to stay up here and work?'

Again Matty nodded. 'Aye.'

'Well.' Willie was grinning widely now. 'Everybody to their own taste, like the woman said as she kissed the cow. But I wouldn't take on a job like this for a pound a minute, honest I wouldn't.'

'I'll do it for half that,' said Matty brightly.

'You won't get much money,' said Joe now. 'I heard Mr Walsh telling your dad. Just over three pounds, and your keep.'

'It'll suit me.' Matty's voice was full of content.

'Goin' to miss you, Matty.' Joe's head was lowered now.

'Me too, Matty.' Willie nodded slowly.

173

Matty looked from one to the other, then said, 'Aw, man, you'll be so taken up with your new jobs you'll forget I exist.'

'No, we won't.' Joe raised his eyes. 'And I tell you what. I'm comin' up here to see you every now and again. Mr Walsh said I could.'

'But not to stay.' This was from Willie. 'Flying visits are all I'm goin' to pay the fells for the rest of me life. Eeh!' He moved his head in wide sweeps. 'When I get back to Shields I'll kneel down an' kiss the bricks outside the station.'

They were laughing all together, Joe with his hand over his mouth trying to suppress his high giggle.

'It's a fact,' said Willie. 'You know, I've learned somethin' from this trip, Matty. People are made different. Do you know that?'

'No kiddin',' said Matty.

'But listen, man,' said Willie, poking his head forward. 'I'm serious. I admit I was mad about coming campin', but I hadn't been here a night afore I knew I wasn't cut out for places like this. I'm honest about it, you see. I'm honest about it, I'm admitting it. Some folks are cut out for the towns, and some for the country. Me, right from the soles of me feet to the roots of me hair, I'm town. An' Joe's the same. Aren't you, Joe?'

Joe lowered his eyes away from Matty's gaze as he admitted dolefully, 'Aye, that's right, Matty, the hills an' things would get on me wick. But' – he brightened up – 'your ma says you're comin' home every other week-end. Eeh! We'll get together and we'll have some fun, eh?' He pushed his fist towards Matty. 'Perhaps you'll get a motor bike, eh? An' then you can scoot home two or three times a week.'

Matty extended his hand and gripped Joe's;

174

then Willie's. They looked at him for a moment longer, then went towards the door, and there Joe, turning, said softly, 'Funny, isn't it. All this happening 'cos you picked Nelson up out of the gutter.' On this he gave Matty a long sorrowful glance, and followed after Willie.

Matty lay quite still. There was a sadness on him now. He would likely see Willie and Joe again; they might meet up once or twice at week-ends, but he knew that something was finished – not just school and leaving his friends, but something bigger that included all that. Yet as he lay the sadness lifted, and there returned to him that strange exciting feeling of joy, and he thought of what Joe had said. He was lying here now because he had picked Nelson out of the gutter, a stray, old, half-blind, dying dog. He could see Nelson now as he had never been able to imagine him since he had died. In front of his closed eyes he saw Nelson young and vigorous, laughing at him, tail wagging, ears alert. Joe had said he could get a motor bike. Yes, perhaps he would have a motor bike sometime in the future, but what he would get one day would be a dog, a dog that was his alone. Like Betsy belonged to Mr Walsh, this dog would belong to him, and he would call it Nelson. Together they would roam the hills. They would go up the hump and into The Bowl. Yes, that was one thing he would do; he would explore The Bowl. He would make sure that in the future, mist or no mist, he would find his way out of that maze of hills and mountains. He would come to know each crag and shape so well that if he was blindfolded he would find his way home. He and his dog, Nelson, would find their way home.

If you would like to receive a Newsletter about our new Children's books, just fill in the coupon below with your name and address (or copy it onto a separate piece of paper if you don't want to spoil your book) and send it to:

The Children's Books Editor
Young Corgi Books
61–63 Uxbridge Road
Ealing
London W5 5SA

Please send me a Children's Newsletter:

Name: ....

Address: ....

....

....

All Children's Books are available at your bookshop or news-agent, or can be ordered from the following address:
Corgi/Bantam Books,
Cash Sales Department,
P.O. Box 11, Falmouth, Cornwall TR10 9EN

Please send a cheque or postal order (no currency) and allow 60p for postage and packing for the first book plus 25p for the second book and 15p for each additional book ordered up to a maximum charge of £1.90 in UK.

B.F.P.O. customers please allow 60p for the first book, 25p for the second book plus 15p per copy for the next 7 books, there-after 9p per book.

Overseas customers, including Eire, please allow £1.25 for postage and packing for the first book, 75p for the second book, and 28p for each subsequent title ordered.